GRACE WALSH

Divine Arrows

Weaving the path of spiritual guidance…

To Stanley

May the arrows continue

to illuminate your path —

Many Divine Blessings!

Grace

July 2014

ISBN: 1-4701-1902-1
ISBN-13: 9781470119027

DEDICATION

This book is dedicated with loving memory and gratitude to my mother;

Amazing Gracie Merrick

In times of silence, she taught me volumes
In times of revelry, she taught me the importance of having fun
In times of challenge, she taught me quiet strength and endurance

In the quiet volumes containing the many revelries of her life, she taught me without saying a word, that sometimes the greatest strength, endurance and courage comes in the recognition of knowing when enough is enough.

~*~

...And to my brother *Bif*

Whose indomitable spirit
Has pointed to a way
A way, which when followed
Became an arrow

And when arrows point
To a higher path
That one trusts
And follows

They become

Divine Arrows

~*~

Contents

Dedication   iii

Blessing   vii

Acknowledgements   ix

Introduction   xiii

Earthen   1

Deep River Woman, Dhrema, Cantilever, Imagine Life, Renewal of View, Queue, Feel, Ada'wehi, Saving Gaia, Reconciliation, Pleiades 11-13, Snow Angel, Lamea's Lament, Alphabet Willow, Linear Niles of Alignment, Cordis Street Avenue, Genealogy

Awakenings   61

Spirit   71

Fairy Dream, Soulstice 21, Art Conjecture, Premier Grande Cru, GODWEB, Zodiac, Quantum Query, Spirit Guide's Breath, Buddha Full, Wickiup, Crossing Guard, Akin of Ten, Helixir of the Gods, Troubadour, Gypsy Folk, Forge On, Transplantformation, Reason, O'Seeker, Yosef

Soul Retrieval   149

Ponderings   161

About the Author   *167*
Arrows of Gratitude   *171*

For all sentient beings

May love and light illuminate your path

Acknowledgements

Books are not usually written without a myriad of family and friends who have inspired them along the way.

To CREATOR, my original source, GREAT SPIRIT and MYSTERY, thank you for my sacred breath and for the divine arrows that never cease to amaze me.

With great gratitude to all of my angels, guides and power animals who continue to watch over me.

To my parents, Amazing Grace and Darvie, thank you for bringing my spirit into physical form; to my sisters Annie, Rita, Moe and Pat, thank you for sharing my life experiences over the years and helping me to grow in so many ways (especially to Annie and Rita for their literary input and edit!); and to my brother David, who's indomitable spirit continues to help pave my spiritual path, thank you for my freedom—for freedom is not free. **SEMPER FI**

To my husband and best friend Bill (Boudreaux), thank you for your endless patience, love and support and for accompanying me on this journey; and to my dear children Jesse and Bill (& his wife Wen) who bring such joy and blessing to my life, thank you for choosing me and for allowing me room to grow alongside you.

Many thanks to all of my varied spiritual teachers for being the divine reflection necessary for my eyes to see—especially Pat and Richard, who first introduced me to the word **'intention'**!; and to the Pathfinder for crossing my path at just the right time with a long awaited reflection of my own painted face—Wado~!

To all of my students, clients and friends who have each brought an added measure of character to my life; especially to Bob, who believed in my voice when I needed to sing—I am truly blessed having known you all, thank you!

To Raven Hail, Iron Buffalo and Lorna Hibbs, many thanks for my Native affirmations. To Brian K., heartfelt gratitude for the red & gold arrow.

To Tracy and Waya, thank you for your spiritual friendship, initial read, inspiration and literal commentaries.

To my ancestors (especially Rachel Harris), the olde ones and all those who have blazed this path before me, thank you for the divine crumbs left along the way! *And to my muse; a most heartfelt gratitude for the privileged reflection of divine weaving...*

With very special gratitude to Kana'ti—for sacred teachings, protection, time never to be done with and the guided journey of allowing me to find my own way...**Yotehay Wah!**

~*~

In addition to the many people who have influenced me over the years are countless books and writings that have equally inspired me. There is much to be said about and even more to be grateful for, the divine arrows of spirit which continue to point a way of guidance for us in the simplest form of words.

Years before I *(remembered)* recognized my image in the mirror, I became a student of and found resonance in a small paperback book and deck of cards that were filled to the brim with arrows, bowls, pipes and stones. These cards have been a daily sustenance and consistent source of inspiration and guidance for me; like a long standing friend *(or perhaps ancestral spirit)* who's wisdom has helped start my every day and who's ancient roadmap have helped make my life choices that much easier...

It is with sincere blessing and volumes of gratitude that I wish to acknowledge and give thanks to *Carol Bridges* for creating *"The Medicine Woman Tarot and Inner Guidebook"*.

Carol's healing art images and medicine woman words of wisdom have painted arrows of affirmation each and every day for me as I have grown and travelled along this spirit oriented path.

So, thank you Carol, for your dedication of ensuring the sacred seeds planted so long ago by the olde ones would continue to spread and sprout amongst those who would recognize themselves in your reflection. Aho!

Introduction

...And so it was, one foggy morning in Hull, that everything became clear. That which had been hidden from view was now as palpable and visible as the low dense clouds forming over the bay. And so she smiled, Buddhakaya in her own right, for her eyes too, had been closed...

When I first began to ponder how I would introduce this book, it seemed only natural that I should first introduce myself—so, *who am I?*

Amused by my thoughts that lead me here, I reflect on a time when I asked myself that very question for 3 days straight. It was part of a weekend workshop called "The Awakening"; an intense, enlightening and profound life changing experience that defined oneself as far as the participant would allow. Even though that was several years ago, it still serves to help me today. As I sit pen to paper, trying to introduce the words you are about to encounter, it occurs to me that they are not just words; they are my story. Up close and personal, these words reside at the center of my soul and for whatever reason, now seems to be the right time to share them with you.

I was a quiet child growing up in the late 50's and early 60's. Looking back, I see those first glimpses of myself beginning to emerge with the arrival of the Beatles. I was 8 years old in 1964 when I fell in love with the fab four and their rock and roll music. I was also intrigued by the sun, the moon and the stars and ever so curious about the deeper meanings of life. I wasn't afraid to seek the answers found in astrology books, tarot cards and all things "supernatural" and seek I did! I guess you could say I was a true child of the universe—and at the tender young age of 8, I was well on my way to becoming a romantic mystic! I learned to sew and before long, my self-embroidered blue jeans became the best expression of myself. *At least that's how things started...*

Then one day on the Ides of March in 1969, life took a different turn. I was 12 years old when the news came that my only brother was killed in action in Vietnam. I remember it like yesterday. Everything comes undone when a death in your family occurs and as a result, a new process of life is forced to begin. Overnight, life became a parody of sorts.

I reverted back to the quiet child, it was easier. My family didn't talk much, if at all, about the war or my brother's ultimate sacrifice. The television got shut off if any news about the war came on. You see it was just too painful. Looking back now I imagine some of this was due to the fact that our country was not only at war in Vietnam, it was at war with itself. The anti-war movement going on during that time left just as many brutal scars and wounds on us families as it did to our returning heroes who unlike today, were often dropped off alone in the middle of the night on some dark back road. In my eyes, I think they missed out on so much more than the simple "Welcome Home" that they at least deserved.

My dad was a retired Marine and must've had a hard time handling this situation. He had survived action in WWII and Korea and had made the Corps his life—surely this had to have been a tough load for even a seasoned Marine like him to carry. Likewise, my mom, a woman of incredible spiritual strength, became an overnight Gold Star mother who never chose to step into that spotlight, for it would've illuminated what surely had to be the worst moment of her life. So coping came with silence; it was the only way.

School was a welcome escape from the house, yet when the school bell rang and I was happily out in the recess playground, my classmates would all be singing anti-war songs. I have such a vivid memory of this- kids laughing, playing, singing words so powerful that I don't think they had any idea how deeply they were cutting me. This so infuriated my grieving soul!

It's easy to say now, that most of them were understandably clueless, as the war hadn't personally touched their lives. Gosh, we were all so young; yet it was one of those life defining times that forges the way you will grow up for it changed us forever; it certainly changed me. At that time, I knew not how to express this dichotomy of my youth, my truth, the state of the world, our world, our family, *my soul...*

I have always felt these emotions on a very deep level and have come to know and appreciate how these intense feelings have shaped my life and my life's purpose. But it would be 31 years before I would take that first *intentional* step towards healing that which was buried so deep within the core of my being and ultimately, that which was also so deeply imbedded within the heart and soul of my family and the Vietnam Veterans who shared the battlefield with my brother David that day.

Life had moved us all in different directions; some of us moving hundreds of miles away from the small town that we grew up in. I got married in 1980, giving up a Computer Science Degree to stay at home and raise my 2 beautiful children. I enjoyed working part time at a local fabric shop and looking back, I can see how this also paved a mending way for the creative expression of my spirit to escape, for it so longed to be freed.

As fate would have it, in 1992 my husband became unemployed and I found myself back to work full time in the same Computer Operations environment that I had once left behind. I spent a lot of time during these years doing genealogical research, trying to prove my Native American ancestral roots. Family rumors had it that my great-grandmother on my dad's side was full-blooded Cherokee.

This had intrigued me ever since I was a very young girl and I would always ask my mom and dad about this but the answers were never quite delivered, for one reason or another. I would come to understand why, many years later. All of the roads in my search led to dead ends. Town halls and records were invariably burned down or lost forever. Then something happened one day. Life turned once again and I have never looked back. Knowing there are no coincidences, only synchronicities, it would soon become obvious to me that the first of my divine arrows had appeared.

We bought our very first computer and I SO loved the idea of "email"! I soon fell in love with the unlimited research capabilities of the internet. Something out there was calling to me and I knew there was one thing I had to do. *What* exactly that was, I wasn't sure yet—but nonetheless, I knew that I had to find out; I was *going* to find out.

There was a passion stirring so deep inside of me, like a driving force from some other place or time. It didn't take long for my internet search to produce results. I found a website called **"The Wall-USA"** which is an online representation of **The Vietnam Memorial Wall** in Washington DC.

Another vivid memory is when I found my brother's name on that virtual wall as I was completely overcome with emotion. So many feelings washed over me; thoughts from many directions came rushing in, totally overwhelming and taking me by surprise. I remember sitting there quietly, allowing these feelings to surface, all the while thinking how I wasn't consciously aware of many of them yet they had obviously been sitting there the whole time, just beneath the surface.

I felt very grateful that there was a small space set aside on this World Wide Web for family members and friends to leave a message for our fallen heroes. It was so good that they remembered and cared enough to do this; and it was *so* good to finally have an opening which would allow some of these old thoughts and feelings to let go. It was September 23, 1999; what would've been David's 50th birthday.

A few months passed and then one day, on the eve of the new millennium, an email popped up in my mailbox. It was from a Vietnam Veteran and fellow Marine who had gone through boot camp in Parris Island with my brother. He had read the post that I left on the Virtual Wall and was moved to write back to me, just to say hello and that he too, *remembered*. I will never forget how he introduced himself to me that day, as my big brother and how he said that there were many more big brothers out there if I chose to meet them that were watching over me and who I could always count on.

He went on to say that there were many websites set up for each of the varied Marine Corps Divisions and if I knew the name of the 'outfit' that David had served in Vietnam with, he would be happy to help me find them. Again, I was so stirred from deep within; a feeling so hard to describe but likened to that of a long lost treasure map being presented to someone after a lifetime of search.

I could only think of one place to find this information; a place that I had always had a hard time going to but soon found myself sitting there at the cemetery sharing these thoughts with my brother as I jotted down the necessary information which would ultimately lead me to what I had been searching for.

A few days later, my boot camp brother sent me the link to the website of my brother's outfit from Vietnam. He even offered guidance as to how I should phrase my message to them. "Keep it short", he said, as many of the guys suffered from PTSD (Post Traumatic Stress Disorder) and it was in everyone's best interest to take things slow. Taking his words to heart, I began to phrase my message as I looked over the mail call link on the website. It was easy enough to find the names of the men who had served in David's company during the same time frame as their service dates were posted alongside their names as well.

I sent out a handful of messages that day, saying who I was and that I was looking to connect with any of my brother's old buds; also wishing them peace in the new millennium. It didn't take long before their responses came back. One in particular was from my brother's Platoon Commander who was there the day my brother died. The Lieutenant went on to share the events of what happened and told me how they had responded to a call for help from fellow Marines when they were fired upon. David and his comrade Tony did not survive.

The date was March 15th and in an eerie twist of fate, it was also Tony's 20th birthday.

As it was/is for so many veterans returning from combat, the Lieutenant had struggled over the years with survivor's guilt, always wondering why he survived this ambush that had taken 2 of his Marine's lives. Ironically, when my email came in, he too had been wondering how to reach the families of his Marines who gave their all during his watch. He had often thought about them and wished to make contact as well. A heartwarming moment for me to know there were others in search of this same treasure map.

It was January 6th, just a few short days into the new millennium—on a day known to some as "Little Christmas" or perhaps better known in the deep recesses of my healing soul as the "Epiphany". I knew this too was no coincidence, yet another synchronicity. I trusted the arrow and followed the way.

Our emails soon turned to phone calls and phone calls to eventual in person visits with each others families. The emails multiplied as more connections were made within the group and I soon found myself at their annual reunions, making new friends, meeting big brothers and most importantly, healing old wounds. I went to Washington DC and visited The Wall. I met my boot camp brother in person on Veterans Day at the Wall and words could never attend to the deeper meanings of our connection nor the multitude of words that went unspoken that day.

My younger sister Annie and I went to David's boot camp platoon reunion in Parris Island where I experienced something so profound that can neither be explained nor denied. The night before I left for this trip, I had a dream. Actually, it was more like a waking dream the morning of. I woke with a song (music) playing in my mind and can attest to the fact that there weren't any radios or televisions on anywhere in the house. This music was quite vivid and was fading out as I was waking up. It was familiar yet I couldn't quite 'pen' the name of it as I attempted to jot this down in my journal.

We spent the next 4 days on Parris Island with a handful of guys who had survived the rigors of boot camp with our brother, back in 1968. It was quite a memorable visit. We met some of their families and got to know their Drill Instructor, who also joined us for this mini reunion. They had set quite an agenda for us. We laughed and cried, ate lunch in the mess hall, took a field trip to the Citadel, witnessed the current 'boot's going through some of the field exercise training and even experienced the intense heat, humidity and bug bites first-hand while the guys recanted the pain of being bit by mosquitoes back then and unable to swat them off while standing at attention!

It was quite the experience just being there with them; watching and listening to them remember certain things and feeling the energy of the place firsthand.

The day that we visited the historical museum (which is right there on base) I remember being impressed watching the "boots" pass us by, marching, proudly carrying their colors. We walked on into the old brick building and as I looked up I noticed there were several rooms upstairs beckoning off of the rotunda. The guys all wandered one way and somehow my sister and I got separated. I found myself climbing the stairs and walked into one of the rooms. They did not appear to be more than single rooms when looking up from down below, yet they snaked way back into the building. The dioramas were laid out in order of Marine Corps battle history. The WWI and II rooms were both downstairs, as I found out afterwards; it seemed I had walked right into the Vietnam Era displays.

I was alone and it was quiet, so quiet you could hear a pin drop. There were maps on the wall, uniforms and weapons laid out just so behind glass displays. The first wall I came to said "1964" as it seemed all the memorabilia was sorted and presented by date. I wandered along the displays, turning corners and being transformed back to another time and place. It was like a time capsule and I was walking through it, though it felt more like I was being led.

1965, 66, 67, 68 all passed me by; uniforms and weapons had obviously changed over the years. I turned another corner and there before me was a giant wall map of Vietnam with the word "DaNang" in big bold letters with a red star next to it. The date above the map seemed three dimensional to me—"1969". I stood there frozen in time just looking at this map when all of a sudden, out of nowhere, music began to play right above my head. Every hair on my arm stood on end and the tears began to fall as the music playing was the very same music in my waking dream just a few short days before. I never moved for fear of it stopping. Instead I opened my heart and tried to just soak it up for all it was worth. I remember standing there afterwards, wondering if perhaps there were sensors at each display that would kick off music appropriate to that time but curiously, no other music had played through any of the previous displays.

I knew without a question of a doubt that my brother had found a way to communicate with me and there was no doubt in my mind what his message was. I stayed there for a few more minutes and after collecting myself, found my way back downstairs where the group was still wandering. It seemed no one had even missed me.

When spiritual affirmations such as this appear, it's important not to let fear get in the way; rather holding onto faith so that we can truly know that they are real. There is so much benefit there for us if we just allow ourselves to experience it, no matter what sense it comes through. We lose so much opportunity when we allow the physical brain to get in the way trying to explain or attempting to doubt. After all, how can something physical ever begin to explain the nature of something so spiritual anyway?

We have an unspoken bond, these Marines and I, as we have both lost a piece of ourselves to that war. We've walked the same walk; different sides of the street perhaps, but the same walk nonetheless.

I knew I had a powerful effect on these men and contributed to their healing process for they were certainly contributing to mine. My deepest intention had always been to ensure they were happy in their lives. It was important for me to know this for they made it home! It didn't make sense to me for it to be otherwise, and besides, I knew David would want them to be happy and find joy in their lives. There was powerful healing medicine at work but I had no idea the true depth of healing that was taking place within my own self.

While walking through downtown Boston on my lunch hour one day, I picked up a free magazine from one of those stands you see along the sidewalk. It was a metaphysical magazine and the front page image had caught my eye. When I opened the cover, I noticed a full page ad for an upcoming workshop called **"The School of Energy Healing".** I signed up that day without blinking an eye, even though the start date was months away. *Funny how these things just spark your soul to life when you encounter them!*

The facilitators interviewed prospective students ahead of time and I remember sitting there in front of them that day when they asked me why I was interested in the class. I told them a little about my experiences in search of my brother and that I knew I had healing capabilities and wanted to fine tune that which I was already doing.

The class was a phenomenal learning experience where we were introduced to the energetics of the body and many different modalities of energy healing. It was an intimate, small group setting of only 10 students and many of us felt like we had done this before. Though we had never met, there was a definite déjà vu that was overwhelming at times, if not downright *fascinating!* One of the facilitators was a Reiki Master Teacher who taught the Traditional Usui Method of Energy Healing.

For those of you who may not know, Reiki is a Japanese presentation of an age-old hands-on healing technique that extends well beyond the days and same practices used by Jesus and Buddha. In its simplest form, a person will feel stress relief and wonderfully relaxed. On a deeper level, it works towards your healing intentions, be they for mind, body or spirit and is complimentary to any other healing modality. It is for anyone and everyone to experience and easy to learn. All one needs to do is open up to the possibility and allow spirit to do the rest.

Over the next few years, I would become her student and follow more arrows that would eventually add my name to the time-honored lineage of Reiki Master Teachers. Reiki has been a natural compliment to my life and I have learned much about myself since I began to study. Our bodies are made up of energy centers, called chakras, and all of our life experiences are imprinted within our energetic self. Every day stresses and health issues add to the imbalance of our energy systems and what reiki does is help to bring our energetic being back into balance. When we set our intentions towards healing there truly are no limits as to what we can accomplish on our path to becoming healthier and happier human beings. Reiki came so natural to me that I began to wonder if I've been doing it all along; either way, I knew my arrows were hard at work.

Yet, all said and done, my native roots still called from a distance. So far away, yet so very near and so very, very deep within the drumbeat of my heart and soul.

By this time, I was actively communicating with several of the guys. My regular posts in their online guestbook led to a message one day from another one of my brother's comrades. His name was Iron Buffalo and not only was he a Marine, but he was also Cherokee. I was drawn to tell him of my native search and he soon put me in touch with his tribal genealogist who in one email, was more than helpful in my quest—not by reason of helping me to find 'proof', but by helping me to see from another perspective. She told me it wasn't the quantity of blood that really mattered—rather what you did with what you had. To this day, whenever I think of those words, they bring me to a place of total stillness. Years of searching and dead ends all fell away in an instant. Right then and there I realized that I did not have to prove anything to anyone, least alone myself; for deep within, my spirit already knew and always had known.

Life around me continued with many interesting twists and turns. In 2006 when I turned 50, my husband gave me a gift certificate towards a week long program called "Earth School" which was held somewhere in the woods of North Carolina. He thought now that I was fifty, I should learn how to make fire without matches. He had won the gift certificate in a raffle during his week of "Bass and Nature Camp"; held in the neighboring woods of Tennessee by the same facilitators (Victor Wooten/Bass Player Extraordinaire and Richard Cleveland/Founder and Director of Earth School).

So off I went to Earth School and the week proved to be an amazing adventure and learning experience that I will not soon forget. I did learn to make fire and among other things, how to survive in nature by identifying edible plants, learning to build a shelter in the woods, track animals and yes even learn to trap and eat them! Perhaps the most memorable moment was the day we built the small animal traps. We had copied the diagrams off the board as Richard was talking and drawing and then each of us went off into the woods by ourselves to gather the materials needed. Being a city girl with little or no camping experience, there were lots of things to overcome including recognizing ticks and how to remove them, avoiding poison ivy, getting comfortable using my knife and believing in myself that I could do all of the above!

I gathered the wood in sacred manner and joined back up with the group as we sat down in a circle to build our traps. The teachers looked on and as I finished Victor was walking up behind me. He said "Wow, Grace, that is perfectly—backwards!!" I think I must've gasped out loud because Vic said something like "No, no it's ok!" I affirmed that it WAS ok as I traveled backwards in my mind, finally understanding why all these years I had never been able to put stuff together. Now I knew why for something inside me translated *backwards!* It was a HUGE "aha" moment for me. Flashes of situations ran through my head the rest of the day…even the long forgotten memory of how some used to call me "Edith"—Edith, being Edith Bunker; as it was obvious to them that my way was very different than most.

As I sit here writing, looking back on this time, I can see how a piece of me was reclaimed that day. I may have recognized it immediately but it would take a few more years before I would truly understand how and where it fit and all the blessings attached with being able to see things the way that I did.

In the meantime, my creative self enjoyed getting back into sewing again and my energy healing practice was beginning to take root. I had visited a labyrinth nearby and found its walking medicine to be mesmerizing, so I decided to search online to see if there were any other labyrinths located in Massachusetts. While searching, I came across a link to a labyrinth in Vermont. I thought I would check it out seeing how we had plans to spend my upcoming birthday week out in the Berkshires, and I was curious to see if this place was within driving distance. It should come as no surprise when I tell you, it just so happens that this labyrinth is part of a Cherokee Buddhist Village devoted to peace and planetary healing. This totally took me by surprise as I thought Cherokee villages were most likely only found in the Carolinas or Oklahoma!

That same feeling came over me again and from that website, I followed a few more links that ultimately led me to an article whose words I soaked up like a long thirsty sponge. Again, there are no words to describe this feeling but while reading this article, the words seemed to jump off the page and embed themselves into the longings of my soul as if the place had been long ready to receive them and they were finally coming home.

I knew I had found my tribe.

The arrows led me to the author's website and an introduction to his new book which had just hit the shelves. Jim "Pathfinder" Ewing is a Cherokee Medicine Man and Reiki Master Shaman Teacher who lives in Lena, Mississippi. I ordered his book on the spot and was not the least bit surprised when I came home from work the very next day to find it in my mailbox. It left me wondering, had I long awaited the book *or had the book been waiting for me?*

This book, called **"Reiki Shamanism"**, is the first of its kind (that I am aware of) which dispels the origins of Reiki as being solely Japanese; instead, shining light on its ancient, native shamanic roots. These words rang so true in my heart that they brought me to tears. I knew, beyond a question of a doubt, that indigenous peoples all over the world had been practicing this type of healing work since the dawn of time. This was also known somewhere deep within my own DNA and had to be the reason it was all so very familiar to me.

I read everything available to read on Jim's website and noticed he was offering an upcoming workshop on Reiki Shamanism within the next few weeks. Without giving it a second thought, I booked my flight and took off to parts unknown, once again trusting the arrows pointing the way before me. That weekend, while sitting across from him in yet another circle of like minded students, the same knowing smile crossed my face as it had a few years previous at Earth School. Jim was talking about the native concept of "heyoka"—a Lakota word referring to the sacred clowns and their healing medicine of being backwards/forwards. Once again my mind raced off in many directions, absorbing yet another "aha" moment as I tied up so many more loose ends of myself, affirming what I had intrinsically known but didn't know at all. And it was heartwarming to say the least, knowing there was a word to describe my backwardness and that it was a native healing word as well!

Jim teaches out of his home in Mississippi, which is 1500 miles away from my own, but ironically, less than a 2 hour drive from the Marine Corps Lieutenant whose contact had been instrumental in setting my divine arrows in motion.

My story pauses here to digress back to the introduction of this book; but I have chosen to share this very personal story with you for it truly is a treasure map of how I found my way. The way is different for each of us just as we are each different from each other. I share my way only as an example, a template of sorts for those of you who may be seeking your own *divine arrows*.

The quiet voice that exists deep in the center of our soul is the driving force that leads us safely through some of the most challenging times in our lives. But we must want to get to know that voice and we must be quiet enough to hear the words when they are spoken to us.

It has been three years now that I have been studying *(remembering)* the old medicine ways under the guidance and love of these teachings with Jim Pathfinder Ewing and his wife Annette Waya Ewing. During this time, many changes, transformations and synchronicities have come about in my personal life. One place in particular had been calling to me, a place that Jim and I visited not too long ago. "Nanih Waiya" is a sacred Indian mound; venerated by the Choctaw as their "Mother Mound" and the place which resides at the center of their creation stories. I found it interesting that this place should cross my path at the center of my own ancestral search; even more so when I learned it was located in Philadelphia—but not the one in Pennsylvania; that would be the birthplace of the United States Marine Corps. *This* Philadelphia is located in Mississippi.

Coincidence? *I shall leave you to ponder this one...*

I read somewhere once that the reason we need spiritual teachers is because the eye cannot see itself; it needs a reflection. Jim's reflection cast back such a powerful image for me that I immediately recognized myself in the words of his book and again while sitting across from him in his workshop. I realized that I had been 'wearing' my medicine (personal power or healing gifts) out on my shirtsleeve as if it were something separate from me—before that I never owned up to this image of myself. It was truly a 'soul retrieval' of sorts for I had to see myself 'out on a limb' before I could finally claim these lost pieces of my soul essence thereby bringing my medicine inward. Being heyoka was indeed a very big part of my medicine. I have always been able to read between the lines, seeing things backward and forward and looking at things in a different way; this was my truest nature...it is who I am. Part of what makes a person an effective healer is being both a mirror and a teacher. All of a sudden, I recognized my own reflection in the mirror. In doing so, I have been able to embrace all aspects of myself. The pieces were all there but I had no reference as to what they looked like as a whole. Powerful medicine when this reflection is cast just by reading someone's words.

The method of my energy healing work and the reserve from which I had drawn had long existed before my first Japanese Reiki class—and I now knew why.

I soon left my state job of 20+ years in order to more fully pursue the divine callings of my heart and soul. The yearnings I once felt towards searching have now shape-shifted into one of learning and *one should never stop learning!*

They say when the student is ready the teacher will appear. I say keep the reflections bouncing! The student is the teacher is the student; as I learn, so I teach. In addition to Reiki/Shamanic healing sessions and Certification classes, I also enjoy offering various spirit-minded workshops. I have learned a lot along the way about a few things and a little along the way about a lot of things—I truly believe there are many more souls out there like me, searching for something as of yet undefined. I wish to be that same reflection for those still seeking as one never knows what will spark that image...

It was no coincidence that out of the blue one day in 2005, I just started writing these words, verses, pages; all divinely inspired and seemingly driven from some other place and time. Dream words, verses of olde, all written long before their divine meanings actually manifested in my life. As the book began to formulate itself, stories unveiled from the present that tied back in to the verses written years previous. Ultimately, these are the pages you will read ahead of each poem…divine testimony to my heyoka medicine! I guess there truly are many healing gifts in the eye that can see backward and forward all at the same time.

So, in answer to the question *"Who am I?"*—I guess you could say I am a Heyoka Medicine Woman and this book reflects the poetic voices and verses of my soul that have been writing themselves out for a very long time.

. . .

Now is a great time of revelation here on Mother Earth. It is no secret that we are living in profound and prophetic times. Indigenous people all over the world are revealing ancient knowledge and sharing their deepest thoughts, prayers and ceremonies of olde. Never before have we been presented with such a wonder full opportunity for healing and reconciliation—but we must be willing participants. Spirit must want out the physical door!

They say a good book holds your attention while you are reading it; a great book holds it long after the last page has been turned. This book has come to mirror my own soul 'awakening'—the soul journey of my spirit and it is my deep and sincere hope that through my words, many of you may discover the treasure maps of your own souls. If these poetic words help to stir, awaken and arouse your curiosity; if your very own and most original voice is enticed to peer on through the veil of perception; if it causes you to take a new look at the collective, conscious movement that is now taking place all across this great land of ours then the waiting of my medicine search would have been worth it.

Dare to look within! Be still enough to listen. Embrace the divine reflection that is being cast out to you.

Just as radio waves perceive the frequency of our favorite music station so that our ears can hear them, so too can your spirit perceive the higher vibrations of the cosmos—the original voice of us all.

Anyone can hear it—*you just have to tune in.*

Many blessings to you all, *most especially* to my warrior brothers of Parris Island Platoon 245 (1968) and the Vietnam Veterans of the Second Battalion First Marines Golf Company, Third Herd (1969) *Hoorah!*
Semper Fi
Grace Walsh
~*~

Nantasket, Massachusetts
2012

Eyes

Windows to the soul

Soul

Doorways to the past

Present

Occurring in the now

Now

It is clear as the crystal

Crystal

Clear the soul for the

Eyes know the way

Back to the future

Past the door to the

Eyes that blink

Drink

From the well

Of

Sacred water

Earthen

~ *Deep River Woman*

~ *Dhrema*

~ *Cantilever*

~ *Imagine Life*

~ *Renewal of View*

~ *Queue*

~ *Feel*

~ *Ada'wehi*

~ *Saving Gaia*

~ *Reconciliation*

~ *Pleiades 11-13*

~ *Snow Angel*

~ *Lamea's Lament*

~ *Alphabet Willow*

~ *Linear Niles of Alignment*

~ *Cordis Street Avenue*

~ *Genealogy*

Deep River Woman

1-1-2006 (A Raven inspiration)

How still the waters run
Deep
Along the Milky Way Path
We are but Souls
Crossing the same river
Great raging river
Across the horizon
We seek sable brown wisdom
Of the mind
It rises
As sacred as smoke
Signals, cosmic secrets
Of the seven directions

Warm in my buffalo robe
Free to love the great wide open
On moonlit mountain tops
She receives communion from the ancestors
Legends of the universe
Speak back the balance
To the vibration of the rainbow
As keeper of the keys
She seeks still
The buried treasure
And you
Fellow traveler of the labyrinth
You navigate the waters
Of this deep river woman

Light me up and open my way!
Your way is Yahweh
Abundance shares freely
Along the White Path of Happiness

Obsidian Shepherd
Ye ask nothing in return
You smoke out my dragons
I salve your soul wounds
As we blaze this trail
Parallel in the traces
The teacher is student
To the friend, the lover
The healer, protector
Transformer of the deep
River Woman

Have you ever had a sense that you've been here before? A Déjà vu? What if one day you woke up and remembered things about yourself that just didn't add up to this lifetime? And then you meditated on it and things began to come back to you. Certain thoughts and experiences became crystal clear.

What would you do? Would you seek the deeper meaning and try to incorporate those thoughts into your daily life?

I believe everything happens for a reason. Timing is everything.

Many years after I had written the following poetic piece, I took a little road trip—all by myself. My husband and I had been visiting with our Marine friends in Tennessee. He got called out to California on a business trip so after dropping him at the Knoxville airport, I decided to drive out to Mt Ida, Arkansas in search of the crystal mountains. I had never been to Arkansas, yet the crystals called to me from afar. Jim and Annette had put me in touch with a friend of theirs who leased one of the local crystal mines and so I booked a motel room nearby and drove. *And drove...*

After 12 long hours I was still driving. By now it was not only dark, but pitch dark on a very curvy country road. Exhausted and beginning to lose my focus, I started to doubt my adventurous self and questioned what I had done. Finally my headlights flashed onto the now dark motel sign and as I turned into the driveway I realized I had overshot it and was about to drive into a ditch. Instincts kicked in and as I slammed on my brakes, the truck behind me (that I had not seen) swerved around me honking and yelling something out his window. With his tail lights now out of view, the night went dark as I put my gears into reverse and pulled up in front of my door. I had called the keeper earlier to say I was going to be late and she told me she would leave the key hanging beside my door. As I cut the engine off, my exhaustion gave way to emotion and I broke down and cried. I grabbed my bag and as I put the key into my lock I noticed something at my feet on the doormat to my room. It was a beautiful black and white feather. I sighed with a smile and picked it up to bring inside.

Come to find out, it was a roadrunner feather! What greater affirmation I thought, could that be? I felt like a roadrunner indeed, beep beeping across the entire state of Tennessee, driving hundreds of miles for hours on end, all alone and ever determined to follow my spirit's calling to a place I had never been.

I was not surprised when I met Julie, the crystal mine keeper the next day, to feel as if we had both met before. She led me up the mountain to dig for crystals but wasn't able to join me as she had to get back to her shop, thereby leaving me there by myself. As she drove off, I will never EVER forget the feeling of being so alone in such a quiet, still remote location. Knowing my sense of direction is usually backwards, I decided to leave my bright orange bucket near the trail to mark my way out. I then started off in search of crystals. I enjoyed the search much more than I ever could've imagined. After meeting my first tarantula and realizing that crystals are amplifiers, I tried really hard to focus on the reason I had been called there. You see, if you allow fear to enter into your mind while standing on a crystal mountain, this fear will grow and amplify and surely drive you mad! *Or at least drive you down off the mountain much sooner than expected...*

As fate would have it, it began to rain and the dark, stormy thunderclouds began to roll in. I weighed out my options and decided to pack up and leave, lest get caught in a Midwestern torrential downpour on top of an unfamiliar mountain whose steep dirt roads may easily wash out.

I shall return one day! This much I *do* know...

Perhaps the old voices are coming back into our conscious awareness as a means to show us a way back, back to a simpler time. Perhaps that will be the revolution, the evolution of our soul. Perhaps we should listen, really listen...to these inner voices and let them amplify and guide us.

After all, they may know us better than we think!

Drhema

12/8/05

Well they said she was a drhema
How could they ever know
The song her heart kept singing
Was the destiny of her soul

She starts out at the beginning
Here at the very end
To understand the nature of things
She could never understand

Drhema Drhema
Meditate your soul
Unfold the crystal vision
Remember the ways of old
(remember the ways of old)

Her light shines across the waters
Like a lighthouse—house of light
Transcend the physical emotions
Trust passionate spirits flight

Bees fly homeward to the hive
Instincts lead the way
Reassurance from the angels
Highest good the only way

Drhema Drhema
Meditate your soul

Unfold the crystal vision
Remember the ways of old
(remember the ways of old)

Kindred spirits bump into the night
Defy time, logic and space
Whispers never to be done with you
My unfounded Amazing Grace

To know the things she does not know
To touch his face unseen
Hold fast to the words she once heard
They complete her snowy scene

Drhema Drhema
Meditate your soul
Unfold the crystal vision
Remember the ways of old
(remember the ways of old)

Drhema Drhema
Unleash your sacred soul
Follow the divine arrows
Back to the days of old
Back to the days of gold
Back to the days once told
Back to the drhema
Rhema
Of old.

...With gratitude for the guidance of the olde ones, as they speak to us to bring back the sacred knowledge of the universe, back from the days of olde, to aid Earth Mother in awakening her people as our destiny unfolds...yes, awaken rhema, for so it was, oh so long ago...

Sometimes I wake up with words on the tip of my tongue. Most times they are so obscure that I have to look them up. Sometimes it happens in the middle of the night and I have to get up to write them down so I don't forget. And sometimes I am inspired to write a verse behind these words, not knowing what half the words that come to me mean, I still write.

This is a great and simple method of self discovery by the way, as many aspects of our selves come through easily in the wee hours of the morning when our brain and physical bodies are sleeping.

"Cantilever" is one of these words.

Long after I had written the following verse, my husband and I were visiting with my Marine Corps brothers and their wives in Tennessee (this is the trip that preceded the Mt Ida adventure). We went to a place called Cades Cove. There, nestled among the Smoky Mountains on hundreds of acres of ancient Native grounds were the remnants of villages from days gone by.

We ventured into a still functioning grist mill and purchased fresh ground corn meal in the gift shop. I fell in love with a particularly LARGE stuffed black bear but decided to think on buying her as she cost more than all of the corn meal available on the shelf that day.

It was raining lightly as we wandered about the grounds. We turned to head back and passed by a rather large barn. As I got closer to it I could see the name on the side. CANTILEVER BARN.
I was drawn to walk inside and looked around, noticing all the girders and beams that defined the 'cantilever'.

Mind you, I had never heard this word before my dream writing it, so it made me smile standing there, in that empty space of the barn as if recognizing something but not quite sure what…

On our way out, I went back into the gift shop and bought that bear.
I couldn't leave her.

She now graces the entry room of my home and answers to the name…
Cantilever…

Cantilever

July 2006

Cantilever show the way
Cross the pines so faraway
Thistles dawn and break the day
Tw'ont be long don't dismay

Away the hark and eagle flies
Ever lasting revelations nigh
Therein lies the way soon found
Trust for thee it shall unbound

For time is essential
Of essence ye'll see
We pick up where left off
Essentially

Cantilever here or behind
She is as one our grace so kind
How sweet the virtues of patience and love
Knowing all in His hands is in order above

A passionate purpose
This season of rhyme
Thyme is the season
An'it's seasoning time

Allow the space to open expand
Invoke the way it points to one man
This culmination of energies so pure
Is our chance to save the world *once more...*

I have always loved the Beatles.

1964 ~ I was 8 years old. My sister Rita and I had matching Beatles tee shirts and we never missed a chance to sit and watch Lawrence Welk or Ed Sullivan with our Nana on her small black and white TV, hoping to catch a glimpse of our Fab Four. We knew all the songs by heart. *Who didn't?*

Those were such sweet innocent times and I will always cherish these early musical memories which I hold so dear to my heart.

Their lyrics so simple yet their musical messages were way ahead of their time. Individually they were equally as brilliant.

"Imagine there's no Heaven, it's easy if you try" (John Lennon, Imagine)

Do you think John was trying to get us to see that Heaven is really here, on Earth?

Even though I had never met George, nor did I ever have the chance to see him in concert, I feel a profound spiritual connection with him. It cannot be put into words although my greatest hope is to one day try to do just that, for his widow Olivia...

Heaven on Earth—what a concept!

Only My Sweet Lord knows for sure...

Imagine Life

12-8-2005 ~ *Ode to George & John* ~
Well let me ask you once again
The words of George & John
What is life about my friend?
How long must war go on?

Imagine a world of peace & joy
When mistakes give way to lessons
When prayers and cries of girls and boys
Fall on ears of a higher impression

Oh seek the deeper meaning my son
Learn from life's true greatest wonders
To see, to hear and taste the rain
In the sun, lightening and thunders

What if we weren't meant to suffer?
What if Love could lead the way?
What if the path were soft, not tougher?
What if peace were here to stay?

Would we see the gift horse with our 3rd eye?
Would we embrace our health and healing?
Though Mother Earth is patient and wise
Father Time's begun his stealing

Oh seek the deeper meaning my friends
Learn now for the time is nigh
Strawberry Fields and Bangladesh
Are still the reason
<u>Why</u>

Life is an onion...and onions make great spirit food for the soul, though they often make us cry.

When you think about it, life really *is* a proverbial onion! All of our life experiences are piled upon each other in our energy fields. Sometimes, when the layer on top is touched by something so sensitive, it resonates way down below to the one on the bottom. Ever have that happen to you? A perfect energy example might be the experience we have whenever we go to a funeral or wake. We get that sense of dread before we even get there because we know it may 'remind' us of another funeral or wake that we had been to; most likely some-one who was very close to us.

Think about how people say "let's get to the bottom of this"...just as there are many energy layers of past experiences hanging on around us, so too are there layers and levels of consciousness available to us to help us heal from old wounds and grow towards the highest and clearest expressions of ourselves.

It takes being honest! If we can honestly look ourselves in the eye and be willing to go through whatever it takes, we *will* get to the bottom of it and on through to the other side.

Some call it the 'dark night of the soul'. Others may refer to it as falling into a dark hole and not being able to get out.

I find it helpful to refer to the onion; because I know ahead of time that it will probably make me cry, and crying is good! It allows for release—for if we don't release that which we hold inside, sooner or later it will build up and find another way to release on its own.

Life is a truly a process; yet it is also an amazing, unbelievable journey.
If you are willing to shift your perceptions, you may just be amazed at this renewed view of you...

"When you are current, your current is strong"
Carol Bridges ~ "The Medicine Woman Inner Guidebook"

Renewal of View

8-21-2007

I don't know about this
The rabbit hole that lies beneath the surface
The one that keeps things so well hidden from view
How did Alice really feel about it??

Salt of the sages
Spicing up my dreams
Transforming refuse
Into spirit golden scenes

Liberation of the soul
Alchemical streams
Salt waters of the universe
Reinforces my seams

Rainbow bridge lights up my way
Regenerating paradise paradoxical stay
That which is hidden shall be brought into view
Casting off excess matter reviving the few

Oh Great Guardian of the Tree of Life
'tis a long road we've been walking in strife
But friends of the mustard seed will heartily agree
We carry each other for we all long to be free

Leaving the lodge our robes change color
Purples go red to green
Leave disruption behind we can now return
To our original, most essential essene

The destruction of matters alchemical state
Renders possible the perfected stone
The mystical philosophical aspects of self
Highly polished, returns home to its throne

So if you get dropped down your rabbit hole
Panic not, just take in the view
Your highly transformed spiriting self awaits
Soul birthing a new illumed you...

I do believe that I have been here before. And I also believe that after this physical body passes away, I will probably be back again.

The following verse entitled "Queue" is much more about the letter for me, than the word. It refers to the recognition of something so profoundly strong and familiar that one cannot put their finger on it.

It is perhaps about the same soul in a different body; or perhaps the same story, different day, or lifetime...

When you think about it, the word queue does evoke a line of sorts; or an image of people standing in line.

Do you think souls stand in line waiting to incarnate?

Makes me wonder why we stand in line at all?
What are we waiting for?

I always come back to my Virgo rationale...there are some things we don't mind standing in line for, other things we would *never* stand in line for...

Makes you wonder...what such thing do people *love* to stand in line for?

Queue

You collect me when I am strewn
Like stones
Endless tumbling in the surf
My once sharp, jagged edges
Now soften, with time

You have always been my fort
My stronghold, my tower
Whenever I have come under siege
Teaching me the value of stillness, breath
And the way ~

A warrior wielding a weaponry of words
Encircling the chuck wagons
You keep them all safe within
As you remain safe, without
The very sight of you
Instills peace in my heart
My safe harbor, my hearth, *home*

I remember…
How many times? So many…

The words still the same, languages change
Spirit speaks louder than words
The veil thins enough to grant me a peek
For I still seek, I forever search, *ever searching*…

Grasshopper came to me today
Quite the leap up to my high window

He waved, got my attention
I know that I am free to go now
And I will
For at long last, I am ready
I am truly free~

So, as my softened self continues
To tumble about in the waters of life
I shall continue to look for you
My collector
My protector
My Q...

Once upon a time, many moons ago and way back when, I intentionally started out on this energy healing journey...

I used to think I had a problem with my voice. You see I have this teeny, tiny crack in my voice that sometimes is more evident than others. Part of why I learned energy healing was to help 'heal' my voice. I even took voice lessons in the hopes of singing that crack away! It took many years of seeking and searching before I finally realized, that teeny, tiny crack was part of who I was. It was just as much a part of me as my deep brown eyes for it defined a very distinct part of myself that was original only unto me. What really needed healing was my lack of owning my truest self!

Feeling is healing and I am well on my way to being done with this healing 'cos I am ready for that feeling!

I think the single and most therapeutic thing we can do for ourselves is to honor ALL of our voices. We tend to stuff our truest feelings, we avoid and escape from our truest thoughts.... Why? *What are we so afraid of?* There is freedom in truth! Have you ever asked yourself *"What is my truth?"*

Oftentimes the weight we carry on our shoulders is weight we place there ourselves. Someone once told me that every problem contains within itself the seed of its own solution. We have within ourselves everything we need to grow, to learn, to expand, and most especially, to heal, to let go, en-lighten and lose the load that we carry.

Our emotions are like steam in a teapot. If we don't open up the lid and let some steam out, the pot will eventually overflow and explode!

So honor all your voices! Let them be heard! They only wish to be released. Once we verbalize them, let them go, most often they are gone for good! What a wonderful gift we can give ourselves if we can only honor this age old adage..."To thine own self, <u>be true</u>".

Go ahead, peel your onion. Ask yourself, *what's bugging you today?*

More than likely, what's REALLY bugging you may not be what you thought at all. But you will never find out if you don't take time to look within, to listen. Self therapy. It's the cheapest date in town! And who knows? *What's buried in that onion may very well be the pearl you've been searching for.*

FEEL

Cream scream
It's all just a dream
Nothing is ever
What it seems

Drown frown
It'll come around
Some days are up
Some days are down

Lift sift
Up thru the fog
Peel back the layers
To get thru the bog

Mind find
Internal control
Show me the path
The great grassy knoll

Strong weak
Only when you speak
Energy impressed
Common ground we seek

Stall fall
Pick up and go
Don't trip on the bump
It's just another hump

Try fly
Separate the two
Physical is dense
Spirit flies with you

Alone on the phone
Why must this be
Such confusion surrounds
Our destiny

Cry oh my
Release it let go
Results would be different
If everything you'd know

Bend send
Your strength back to me
Wrap me and hold me
Your embrace sets me free

Extension suspension
A mystery unfolds
Unveiling a prophecy
From days of olde

Crazy insane
A masquerade of mind
Deceptive intelligence
So very unkind

Awake don't forsake
Don't give up on me now
Still trust it will be
If ye don't know how

Alive contrive
The way back is thru
You know this, remember
I am struggling too

Peace cease
To question what's true
You softened my heart
It opened for you

Bring sing
Those songs just for me
My soul longs to hear
Your heartstrings in G

Mend send
Those notes from afar
Surround me your light
Emissary of star

A dove of love
Alight in my space
Surrender serenity's
Sweet divine grace

Be still to fill
Nose to toes
For what's written in stone
Heaven only knows

Ok I am thru
Done with no fun
Nowhere to hide
Nowhere to run

Accept the concept
No one else knows
A select chosen few
Know the king is a Jew

Beguile a while
Rest easy I say
You have what it takes
Survive the earthquakes

Lay down and rest
Your weary head now
My lap's in the sky
Star blankets we lie

When you wake from the dream
It will all make sense
Be content and just be
It will set you free

A promise never breaks
Twin souls never part
For love is forever
Cast in a purple heart…

Many moons ago, an olde friend sent me a newspaper article that really piqued my geneological interest. It referred to a book about the olde ways of the Cherokee and their ancient tradition of finding your natal day sign. Having been on a quest for some time searching out my native roots, I was fascinated from the first browse and began to follow links to purchase it.

Finding only a snail mail address and phone number, I decided to pick up the phone and call my order in. An elderly voice answered and I knew immediately it was the author herself! She was slightly amused by my shock and we went on to share a wonderful and most memorable conversation.

Knowing there are no coincidences, only synchronicities, it came out in the conversation that the city she lived in was the same city I was planning to visit within the next few weeks. I decided to step out on a limb and asked if she would mind if I picked the book up in person. She graciously obliged asking only to keep her address confidential and before long I found myself sitting in her living room talking about life. She told me of her struggling health and since I had just recently learned Reiki, I offered to give her a healing session which she accepted without blinking an eye. After the session, she told me that she didn't know anything about Reiki but what she did know was what I had just done was not Japanese.

She has since passed on but her words will forever live in my heart. I framed the page of the book that she signed that day and have it hanging on the wall in my studio. It reads "To the promising Medicine Woman"...*(hmm, wonder what I promised?)*..."May the Great Spirit make sunrise in your heart!".

I stepped into my higher calling that day but it would be several years before I would fully integrate those words into my mind, body and spirit.

Life is short so don't be afraid to take chances! How will we ever taste the blessed fruit if we are not willing to step out on that limb? I walked away with so much more than a book that day and will never regret or forget how I found the author and wound up spending an afternoon at her house exchanging sacred gifts.

Wado Saho'ni

~*~

Ada'wehi

(Cherokee: Healer)
12-10-2005

She speaks the language of the birds
heard high above the mountain tops
she paints the colors never heard
redefines the circle crops

Come minion of the moon tonight
be still my heart, be still
the healing stirs from deep within
to save your soul at will

Eagle flies a lonely path
to see with crystal vision
pave the way and stay on track
the universal mission

Oh Great Spirit, guide
the Shaman of the Lodge
speak wisdom of the universe
there's no place left to dodge

Falling stars upon the night
ancient reflections of myrrh
far and wide across the sky
the Great Buddhakaya stirs

Come minion of the moon tonight
the warming fire waits
the blessings of the universe
begin at Heaven's Gates....

One of the first things I learned, if not the first, when I was a student at the **"School of Energy Healing"** at the **Open Doors Metaphysical Gift and Learning Center** in Braintree, Massachusetts, was that intention is everything. "Intention", Richard said pensively, *"remember that word."*

Little did I know how much that word would become a part of my daily life.

Nowadays, as a part of my own healing practice, I teach others about the power of intention. The words of my book and poetry affirm it—when we set our minds to do something there is nothing that cannot be accomplished; but, we must be willing participants!

Energy follows thought and thought follows intention.
We truly are what we think!

To give you an example, how many times have you encountered a miserably unhappy person, be it at the office or in a social situation. You walk into that room and their misery is palpable! Why is that? They are literally drowning in their own miserable thoughts. Those thoughts are the only ones that they are allowing in and the more they think them, the more they grow. The energy that they emit is a reflection of what they are thinking. Misery!

They could think happier thoughts if they stopped being miserable long enough or if they chose to, but they have obviously not made that their choice; certainly not their intention.

So you see, energy follows thought which follows intention.

You may have heard the expression "collective consciousness". People all over the world are finding ways to live simpler, be more energy efficient, live more in harmony with nature. Let's face it, if we are not part of the solution, we are part of the problem. We cannot be both.

Now is the time foretold by our ancestors and the ancients as a time of great change. Mankind has made great strides in the way of technology and industry, yet many of these ways are now leading to our demise. As a good friend would say: "We have progessed to the point of digression". In order for human beings to progress and survive these earth changes we must be willing to leave those old ways behind and set new intentions for ourselves, first individually and then collectively. So you see, one person really *does* make a difference. How you think, what you think, not only affects you—it affects our future.

Saving Gaia

5-18-2007

If you dare to believe I tell you it's true
Dare to bring your destiny through
Believe you can step through the flaming door
Physical plays some but spirit offers so much more

Set your intention—believe in this too
For highest good only it will render due
Act as if it's already happening today
Walk the sacred path for on this you must stay

Honor Mother Earth and all her life forms too
Take only what you need & pay respect all the way thru
Believe the world can change, help us show them how
Gaia's Earth needs saving, so wake up! The time is now!

Close your eyes to see, her beauty's all around
Tune down your ears to hear nature's symphony of sound
Once upon a time there was balance—this balance we must restore
Send it out from your heart place, peace and love forevermore

For in the absence of time and space all reverts back to the ONE
We are all intrinsically connected when separate illusions come undone
Our collective unconscious can create the world anew; this process
        underway
As we begin to reclaim our heritage
For Gaia's Earth
Is here to stay...

Checkbooks and checkpoints
Accounts along the way
Progress and egress
Agreements here to stay
Reconcile your money
Harmonize your funds
But what about your spirit
What keeps that from coming undone?

Many aspects of my self have changed along the way while on this path of healing. The mind, body and spirit all have to keep up and re-align as you go in order to keep the balance. I suppose it's the same with any other learning in life, one naturally adapts as you progress so you can grow and integrate the infusion of new knowledge. Just as athletes bodies physically adjust during times of training, so too does the energy worker have to adjust as their vibratory rate changes. What that means is, when we 'lighten up', we are truly doing just that. Letting go of what no longer serves us...

Many energy workers are also referred to as "lightworkers" which can be translated a few different ways. We willingly go through the refiners' fire, so to speak.

It ain't easy being human!

We struggle, we strive and we endure.

Along my way, there were many days when I was complete and happy in my own little space. I could've stayed there but my spirit wanted me to push on. And there were also many days that I got frustrated, depressed and felt like throwing in the towel. But it was okay for me on those days because I knew somewhere deep within me, I had saved up a teeny, tiny reminder—that no matter how tough things might be, it was going to be okay. It really was.

It's good to know that we don't need much in the way of this reminder ~ for the tiniest bit of it will do. And believe me, I remember, some days that was even hard to find!

Today, neither money nor love can ever fill that space for me, the one that I save for my toughest of times ~ only this tiny kernel of spiritual seed; it's all that I need. It's all anyone needs.

After all, our spiritual savings account is the only one that really matters in the end...

Reconciliation

Like the pupil of my eye
I see and study myself
My shadow self
And into the light I shine
Cast like a beacon
This providence of light
So divine...

I do it for me
If not, then who?
I am the only one
Who can get me thru

Be gentle and sit
With yourself for awhile
Create a peaceful space
Whatever your style
Be honest and look
Thy own self be true
Soul searching requires
Spirit food just for you

Be quiet and still
Let your own love light shine
It connects to the Source
Of one great big divine
Peace can be found
When you close the outside door

It's all up to you—nothing more

You have what it takes
To get to the other side
But you must be willing
To go along for the ride

I do it for me
If not, then who?
I am the only one
Who can get me thru

Be willing to go through
Whatever it takes
The prize you will win
Heaven's highest stakes

First locate then clear
Your cobwebs and dust
You may sneeze for awhile
But this way you must trust

To brush out of the old
Makes way for the new
For in this emptiness lies
The real essence of you...

Ever since I was a young girl, I have been staring up at a certain group of stars in the night sky. I don't know exactly when this practice started, but it always gave me great comfort, a protection of sorts, whenever I would spot them. I called these stars my "question mark".

To this day, I have to look up and find my question mark. And the funny thing is that I usually spot it right above my house!

Ironic that something labeled in my mind as a 'question mark' could represent and imply such a definitive, yet non-verbal symbolism for me—a dichotomy of sorts. Knowing but not knowing; something understood yet not understood at all. Just that deep feeling of knowing when you experience something so profound with no questions asked.

Perhaps I always knew the answer—and just needed to find the ?

(It would be many years before I would learn (remember) that the Cherokee consider the Pleiades their home...)

Pleiades 11-13

(for Jesse & Rita)

Seven sisters spinning
Lottery tickets winning
Around the world in seven days
Guide the labyrinth of maize

Grandmother's star arrives in time
Lending poetic reason and rhyme
September men who mentor few
Spear heading arrows point back for you

Awakening up at the helm
Stern holding upon the wheel
Time and space are standing still
A compass encircles surreal

Ships in time that mystically evolved
Wash up mysteries waiting to be solved
Eyes of the ancients etched in windows stained with glass
White masquerading horses polish bridles edged in brass

Beams of light penetrate the darkened atmosphere
Shadows cast across the sky inviting faith and fear
Seven sisters spinning will crest the moon once more
And deep the roots of humble pie knocking at the door

Headings of the universe finally back on track
Celestial sails now filled, wind ever at our back
Settle down, relax and trust the guidance based on love
For the nautical maps of olde were cast from skies above...

I love the snow. It's fresh, pure, clean, soft…

And I love making snow angels, it's like lying down on clean, fresh sheets of linen.

In my dreams sometimes I go to my imaginary place. It's my very own place of pure thought. It's white like snow there but it's never cold.

I go there in my mind whenever I need to get away, rest or recharge. Sometimes in the whims of my wildest dreams, I imagine there are others who join me there.

I liken it to the light, *divine light.*

Imagine what it would be like to stand underneath a beam of GOD's pure, white light, knowing that each and every particle shining down on you was infusing your soul, cleansing your spirit and recharging you from the inside out.

Perhaps I go there for clarity, for if the quantum particles of snow are really just ice crystals, then it would make sense for things to become crystal clear while I am there.

Having grown up in New England, I know that most of us have surely tasted snow as kids. But how many of us have ever listened to the snow?

Listened, to the snow?

"Angels can fly because they take themselves lightly…"
~ Gilbert K. Chesterton

Snow Angel

1-8-2006

Snow falling soft
The angels embrace
And welcome you back
To our safe snowy place

The years come and go
The days they drift pass
The love it still grows
I watch it amass

Your feathers grow back
Your wings they unfurl
Fly back to the place
Of oysters and pearls

For webs they are many
Some stick and some pull
Yet all serve a purpose
To teach us in full

Stay not with the spider
For the web holds too tight
Click one up the lens
To the place of white light

Where the eagle soars free
High and into the night
And sings songs of your wings
Of your strength and your might

Fly home to the land
Of snow and pure thought
Where angels remember
What once was forgot

The Promise of Life
The Renewal of Time
And poetry of wings
Snow angel of mine…

Desires lead to fantasies

Fantasies lead to dreams

Dreams lead to possibilities

Possibilities become realities

Realities become the possibility that dreams awaken in fantasies if we only tap into our desires—and yearn for more...

"The best antidote I have found is to yearn for something. As long as you yearn, you can't congeal: there is a forward motion to yearning."
~Gail Godwin

Lamea's Lament

4-19-2007

Passionate my spirit
So deep and so wide
Opens me up from so deep inside
Fathoms of the sea
Depths of my heart
Feelings atrophy
When spirits fall apart

Her seamstress mends the way
Her healer salves the wound
Her lover sparks the flames
Of passion from the womb

Go with the flow
High and low the tide
Time is a healer
Pain will always subside
Aim for the sky
Let the arrows lead the way
Chaos comes along
But SPIRITS here to stay

Trust the greater plan
Still works for you and me
Highest good the only way
FAITH will set us free
To float amongst the heavenly clouds
Drift softly along the shore

This taste so sweet as honey
Leaves me always wanting more

Transcend the physical barriers
His best advice to me
The spirit doorways open
But your mirror I cannot see

Losing is not an option
The way will come around
My faith is grace unspoken
My love it knows no bounds

This space I hold for silver
Will meld one day the sun
For the treasures of the universe
Are ours *thy will be done* ~

"Communing with nature"—*what does that really mean?*

One night I came home from work to find my neighbors cutting down their weeping willow tree. I'm talking a huge, gorgeous willow that *had* to be at least a hundred years old.

I ran into my back yard to get a better view. All of a sudden I found myself talking to her, consoling her. Mind you, I had never 'talked' to this tree before but there was an urgency in my words, like I had to get them all out before it was too late. My eyes darted from the sky to her limbs, to the crane that carried her huge branches across the yard and over to a truck where they separated the smaller branches, some going immediately into a huge mulcher.

I brought my hands into prayer position bowing my head, in deep reverence and started to pray. I acknowledged how much we enjoyed seeing her dancing in the wind and how the kids loved to play with her wispy branches that often blew over into our yard. I talked about the crows and how I always used to notice them sitting high up on her limbs. I thanked her for being there so strong and so beautiful for so many years...I told her how I could always spot my house when the flight pattern flew over our town because the huge tree always stood out. And I said I was sorry for not recognizing her like this before.

The conversation was very intimate, emotional and moving. It took me by total surprise.

I don't exactly know what she stirred up in me, but the visual of her being cut down had an immediate and stunning effect.

After all the trucks left, I wandered down the street staring in quiet disbelief. The neighbors had all gone in and I stood there alone. Looking down, I found a lonely wisp of leaves lying there on the ground. I picked it up, smiling as I hugged it close to my heart. I thanked her for the everlasting gift one more time. I brought the little branch home and sealed it in a large plastic bag. I shall try to preserve a few of her leaves and perhaps frame them along with a verse from my inspired poem.

Tonight when you go home, take a look around your neighborhood. Ask yourself what you would miss if one day you came home to find it gone.

Because sometimes the things that have the most influence on us often go unseen, unnoticed...

Alphabet Willow

(for Joleen)

Weep not my willow
For I weep for thee
My blessed friend
And sacred tree

Your arms they stretch
So far and wide
I've never known you
Not by my side

The children grew and oft they played
Underneath your cascading shade
Such a sweet and gentle wind swept
breeze
Always blowing the leaves from your
trees

Weep not my willow
I'll weep for thee
Your footprint remains
A spiritual tree

How great the ravens atop your perch
How empty the sky as you they search
But times they change, things come
and go
Why they cut you down, I'll never
know

A recycle bin comes to claim you now
From dust you were, back to dust you
now go
I stare in disbelief as the shredding begins
I bow to your majesty much to my
chagrin

Weep not my willow
My existential friend
Your limbs they're still great
Your arms they'll always bend

Dig deep in the earth for your roots
are so strong
Still sway in the breeze you're protection I'll so long
And hold close many thoughts from oh
so long ago
With gratitude I bless thee, for your
loss, I do know

Your trunk once so great, so wide and
so tall
Now being shred into mulch oh so
small
Your essence it stays, only changing
with the view
A new home you'll adorn, your next
life's coming thru

Weep not my willow
For I weep for thee
My blessed friend
Most sacred tree

O'er the years I've admired your great
stature and stance
Always loved watching your graceful
green dance
If I've never told you then please hear
me now
I am blessed by your presence, in hon-
or to you I now bow

As they take down and away my back
yard view
Know I will never forget, nor render
you through
Your wisdom will always blow gentle
in the wind
My eyes ever behold my green dancing
friend

Weep not my willow
Let me cry for thee
Let my tears of transition
Ever change you, set you free...

-Ancestors—Elders—Old Ones -

-

All who have gone before us have left us with their legacy. Be it a word, a thought, an action ~ some we are conscious of, some not. Perhaps they left us a visible offering of themselves; something physical that was bequeathed to us...

How do we relate to this inheritance?

Do we relate to it?

Spirit food for thought:

All that has gone before us has returned to the ashes of the earth.
You could say the earth is alive with the consciousness of our ancestors.

The earth is also alive with our daily sustenance of fruits, vegetables, grains...

This is the cycle/circle of life.

Something to consider, the next time you prepare to say grace ~
a verbiage of this lineage...

"When things are lined up properly, all sorts of good stuff just happens"
~A.T. Stevens Jr.

Linear Niles of Alignment

Tough tacks and they will prick
But the rose smells ever sweeter
As the scent traverses the saltwaters of love

Mine throat is as parched as the desert sands
That separate the distance of far off lands
For wheneth the voice is unspoken and dry
'Tis only reflecting the nakedness of eye

Alone am I when I'm not with HU
Spirit spotted pleasures, so real yet so few
You cannot see the quench of thirst I have known
When eyes wide shut have taken the throne

Be still and feel the rivers on rise
The momentous occasions will be a surprise
To sense the arrival of the supplicants day
Rendering the passions of a splendoring play

A pie in the eye a slap in the face
Nothing compares to God's divine grace
A sheltering, sweltering shocker or three
Unloads the weight of our destiny

If now it's too hard to see thru the pain
The blessings in disguise, the things we will gain
Know time is a healer and won't compromise
For the heart holding truth shall soon realize

Lines are drawn and ways do part
Love is not only of the heart
But soul and saviors save the day
Soldiers fight to win the way

Commit don't submit to the pension of pound
Release the magnanimous colours of sound
Forein is the mention of mothers who prayed
And live to see their rainbows forayed

Amend the part where the crease is bound
Feel out the sounds of melodies round
For capturing the essence of making array
Is to be the second coming *of this glorious day…*

Funny what you remember about the house you grew up in.

I remember the crooked back steps, the old pulley clothesline and the red enamel painted walls in our bedroom that we used to chalk on. Oh, what fun that was!

Our front steps were like an alcove which always made for great hide and seek places as well as a protected 'stoop' to sit on outside during inclement weather.

We also had 2 doors leading into our apartment, one right across from the other, which was quite the unusual layout.

Our address was certainly different than anyone else I knew. Most folks either live on a 'street' or an 'avenue' yet our address encompassed both. Not sure why but whoever was in charge of street naming that day must've thought it was a good idea. I suppose it was as it did set us aside from the rest; although I'm sure it drove the mailman and post office mad!

Interesting to note, some 40 years and several moves later, the door number that graces my front door today is the very same number that graced our door way back then.

So, what's in an address anyway?

Webster's might define "address" as a written message or a specific memory location or maybe just a destination and quite possibly, one that we are all going to get to sooner or later, *no matter where we live...*

Cordis Street Avenue

Clark bars and hockey sticks
Rooms that lie between betwixt
Guitars and rugs and closet doors
Monsters under the bed forevermore

Passageways of time and space
Allow the touch of amazing grace
Windmills, sions, vehicles of the day
And diamonds on fingers pave the way

Where is this house in New Orleans?
And why is nothing as it seems
Nineteen is such a very young age
To cash in the chips and become a sage

Who is the man whose nickname is Bif?
Returning to dust and acting as if
The temple on the mount were just a school
Did Solomon and the Templars have us all fooled?

Hockey and candy and teeth needing time
Easter bonnets in monumental pictures of mine
Walk along high streets so innocent so young
In the blink of an eye it all comes undone

Weddings and funerals and children askew
Messages calling me back to you
Search out the men who hold the key
All ways faith full to remember me

Connecting the sun to the Mother of Light
Patiently knowing it will be alright
Holding hands they take up the way

Guardians of Heaven *watch over us today*...

"...times they are a'changin"...(Bob Dylan*)*

How many times have we heard "the more things change the more they stay the same"? What really stays the same?

What really changes??

When I think of my Mom and Dad, I wonder how it must've been for them growing up as children and then what it was like emerging out into young adulthood during the depression years; how they met, married, struggled and endured over the years. I think about how my own life experiences and transitional times seem so very different from theirs. I imagine their parent's journeys as well as my own children's journeys were/are and will all be equally different.

Yet in some ways, *they are very much the same...*

It's good to know who our ancestors are/were. I always find it interesting when corresponding and significant dates and names overlap with our own present day ones. For instance, take my great grandmother whom I've never met yet feel an uncanny connection with; she died exactly 10 years prior to the very day that I was born! These kinds of things always peak my interest as I know there are no coincidences in life...The system of numbers is a science unto itself and one that equally connects us on many levels. I've always had a fascination and certain intuitive interpretation when it comes to numbers. I believe that we all came here for a reason—so if this was known ahead of time, what we came here to do, then the numbers defining our unique template would surely have to add up.

But—only if we looked at it from this perspective.

If you've never endeavored a genealogical research on the internet, then maybe you're lucky enough like me and have a family genealogist who works tirelessly, selflessly and with inspired reverent interest, to document, reveal and share all of the connecting limbs on your family heritage tree. Yes, if you're really lucky, you too will have a very special cousin like I do.

This one's for you cousin...

Genealogy

(For Frank)

Family first
On this family tree
Frank's written it all down
Just for you and for me

Ancestral lineage
Age old names to see
Grandmothers and fathers
From way o'er the sea

How we all got here
Begotten of who
Be it a Merrick or Connolly
Or Collins or Pugh

He's done all the work
The lineage unfolds
To honor their spirit
Their memories of olde

How they all worked so hard
To provide us a way
Some lived and some died
And some even went astray

But the tie that binds us
Is one that never breaks
For the fruit of our limbs

Is all the remembrance that it takes...

Awakenings

As I look back over the many footsteps which have led me to this place, I am reminded just how much I have always been in tune with my spiritual self. I'm not really sure when it all started or when I became aware of it, but I do know that I was pretty young.

I can remember a few times in the 1st or 2nd grade, when I would "run away" for the day; walking just a few short blocks from our house to sit for hours on end in the back of St. Mary's Church in Charlestown. It was always on a Saturday, after my chores were done and I had collected my weekly allowance of thirty five cents from my dad. *(I remember this because he would give my older sister one dollar; she would take fifty cents, give me thirty five and my younger sister, fifteen. That bought a lot of penny candy in those days!!)*

I would sit quietly, in the pews at St. Mary's Church, all by myself and quite content and peaceful. I can still see myself, sitting there as if I were communing with someone, *something*. People came and went, saying their prayers, lighting candles. Funny, on Sundays when it came time to go to church, I would often spend the hour in our local coffee shop spending the collection money on a vanilla coke and a bag of chips! After mass was over, I would usually slip into the back of the church to retrieve a church bulletin which I proudly brought home as proof of my attendance. I guess even at this tender young age, I was expressing my spiritual self in my own way! I have very vivid memories of this.

This was around the same time that I saw a UFO. I can remember the exact location where I was standing when it happened; most likely I was walking home from the playground which was just a few blocks from the church.

It was big and silver and round, hovering very low to the ground with lots of bright flashing lights, just as one would imagine it to look like. My memory of this occurrence is of myself standing there in awe and then thinking, *where did it go?* It was there and then it was gone, in what seemed to be the blink of an eye. I remember looking around at people to see if anyone else had noticed. It seemed they hadn't. I don't think I ever told anybody, but I never, ever forgot it. This imprinted memory is quite vivid and still clear as the day it happened.

Across the street from where we lived was an elderly woman named Mrs. Rose. We used to visit her and run her errands and sometimes my sister and I would take turns sleeping over to keep her company. I used to see ghosts in her house but never thought much about it; I just accepted it as the way it was which is the really great thing about kids—they are open to these things; innocent and still connected to spirit by nature of their youth. Maybe to kids, these things seem 'normal'. Makes sense, because it isn't really until we grow older that we become conditioned by all the belief systems being taught to us that we lose this innocent and natural spirit connection. What we 'learn' in life as we grow up tends to take the place of what we once 'knew' as youngsters.

Something else I remember about myself at this age was that I always talked about wanting to go to Peru. Kind of an odd request for a kid to make, especially since I was never exposed to any information about it; yet I remember always saying it to different people, *that I wanted to go to Peru.*

When I was 13 or 14, my older sister and I both saw the same ghost in her apartment. That was kind of creepy as the doorbell used to ring in the middle of the night and 'someone' would buzz the door open. I say 'someone' because she lived on the 2nd floor and was the only tenant in a 3 family house. I used to sleep over because her husband worked the 3rd shift and she was afraid to stay there alone. I soon found out why! We would hear footsteps coming up the stairs that would eventually come to stop outside her door.

We were both certain each other were asleep one night, when the face of an old man appeared above us. He had the face of an old sea captain and it was floating in the air over us, as we lay in the bed. He looked down at each of us, his gaze long and slow from one to the other and then he moved slowly past us, right on through the wall. I never felt threatened, apparently my sister didn't either as neither one of us said a word until the morning when we each shared the same description. He showed up a few different times. She moved out of that house soon thereafter and I don't think anyone has lived there since!

I've had several other 'supernatural' experiences over the years and have come to embrace them as just that—super natural. Think about it, if our 'physical' life is what most of us think is 'natural', then I would have to believe our 'spiritual' life is 'super' natural. I have always believed and resonated with this unseen world and have come to know it exists in part for us to learn and be guided from.

It seems many people these days are gravitating towards life on a more spiritual plane. As world conditions continue to change, many folks are seeking answers from increasingly popular spiritually minded activities. Yoga, tai chi, meditation, Reiki and the healing arts are all of a sudden enjoying a renewed interest; but they are far from new. Likewise, 'new age' is just a current presentation of that which has long been established. It serves us Westerners well when we incorporate some of these Eastern practices into our daily lives; for they bring a much needed balance to our mind/body/spirit.

Knowing that everything happens for a reason, it comes as no surprise that my Reiki training would further amplify these natural spiritual attunements for me. In that light, I share these stories and this poetry with you in the hopes that it may inspire and encourage anyone who may have had similar experiences to perhaps seek the deeper meanings and find out which way these 'divine arrows' may have been or are pointing for you.

Having said all this, I would like to share with you one of the most incredible experiences of my life. For those of you who may still have your doubts, I invite you, just for today, to leave any preconceptions at the door and thereby allow your spirit the freedom to read these words vicariously through my eyes...

...It was late fall/early winter time in New England, back in 2001. I was awakened one night from a seemingly sound sleep when I sat straight up in my bed feeling as if someone or something had literally "dropped" me from the sky. Like the image of Dorothy falling from the tornado bound house in the sky of Oz, back down into her bed. Similarly, she too was jarred awake, sitting straight up as startled as I was. I remember the sensation well, that feeling of falling as if it had just happened and how I woke right up upon impact. It was 4 a.m.

I had no recollection of 'where' I had been; only a knowing that I had been *somewhere* and must've woken myself up when I came back. I had once read about 'astral traveling' but mostly only ever associated it with the enlightened Buddha's of the Far East. It had never occurred to me that this was something I could do, *or did do*. The possibility of it makes sense though, during our sleeping hours that our spirits are free to roam. If you think about how we daydream, don't our minds rest while our spirits travel off to other places? I suppose it is really no different then, only at night, our physical minds, brains are resting and not (fully) conscious. *Who knows where our spirits really go while we sleep?* Perhaps they go 'home' to re-charge or off to 'Spirit School' *(as my Reiki teacher Pat would say)* to learn something important and bring it back for when we awake. Now, there's a thought!

In hindsight, I realize (real eyes) now that I *was* astral traveling and that I woke up during my spirit's 're-entry' into my physical body. It's a weird sensation and hard to describe; like running out the door to go somewhere and slamming smack dab into yourself as you are also running into the house at the same time.

Maybe this was my first time and the reason I woke up, for I remember other experiences since when I haven't woken up. Still, at the time, it both amazed and terrified me.

As time went by, each night before falling asleep I started noticing gentle, swirling lights. I was so mesmerized by their luminous dance of light. In my mind's eye I would watch them. They would always come and go just as I was about to drift off, behind closed eyes. I once asked my spiritual teacher about it and he told me they were 'olde friends', coming to say hello. Well, that thought not only intrigued me but it also warmed my heart!

Many nights came and went as I watched them dance. My inquisitive self often wondered what lay beyond them and if I could get to the other side for a look? And then it happened…

It was as if a window had opened and I had slipped on through. I found myself floating in space, with the great cosmic expanse of universe spread out before me. I could not "see" myself as there was no *physical* form to see. Rather, I was more of an imprint, a thought, an energetic presence. I was not visible to the eye yet fully present in consciousness. I did not venture far as I had the distinct impression of needing to just 'hang back' and watch. *What*, I would watch, I had no idea. *How* I knew this, I also had no idea.

Funny thing about spirit travel while you are sleeping is, you trust. Makes sense, since your physical brain is asleep, there is no physical questioning going on. Only a pure, sincere spiritual knowing that is undeniable and very, very real.

In retrospect, I see now that I was just 'being'. I was experiencing myself in pure spirit form as my physical body lay sleeping. *(Imagine what our amazing spirits might accomplish if we only quieted our brains more often!)*

As I floated in silence and stillness, I noticed something moving towards me from a distance. It was a small bit of energy, akin to myself, not visible but present, and it was moving slowly across the horizon in my direction. I found myself ever so slowly moving towards it, as if drawn to it magnetically and in total awe.

(Even now, years later, trying to put this experience into words is so hard to do; for the immensity of this moment just cannot be translated sufficient to words.)

My 'impression' of this energy was it was also experiencing some great sense of awe. If 'it' had a face, I would liken the expression to that of a small child standing beneath it's first Christmas tree looking up at all the splendor and lights and magic that takes ones imagination and breath away. The recognition of this energy form was immediate; even though 'it' was pure energetic dust and not a physical form at all.

In my mind's ear, I heard myself say "It's George Harrison!"

As my spirit brushed up against his *(a cosmic hello of sorts?),* I noticed in the distance a rather large energy source swirling towards us. At that moment, I knew I did not belong there and that I had to get back. The impression was one of bowing down and out and I felt myself pulling back and away with my head lowered in reverence. As I closed my eyes, I noticed the larger swirl of energy had joined up with George and was now swirling away from me. I remember smiling, thinking I had gotten 'back' in time and the feeling of awe, knowing that the look on George's 'face' was one of great wonder and amazement too.

I woke right up and my physical brain soon kicked in. I was so shaken and out of breath that I had to wake my husband up too. "Wake up, wake up" I remember telling him. It was in the wee hours of the night so he only half opened his eyes to look at me. The words came without a thought *"George Harrison is dead!"*

You can well imagine the look on my husband's face as he tried to figure out what the heck I was talking about and why, at this early hour of the morning. To his credit, he did sit up and listen to me and I was grateful, as I felt the imperative need to tell him everything before my feet even hit the floor. He listened pretty attentively for someone who had just been roused from a deep sleep, until I finished sharing my 'dream'. By the time I finished, he was speechless, half lying and half sitting there in disbelief, not finding any words to say other than "*wow*".

At this point, I had to get up as sleep was no longer an option. I walked out into the living room and clicked the television on. Mind you, I never watch TV and gave up watching the news as well as reading newspapers long ago. So I have no idea why I even did this.

Before the picture even came up, the music was audible...

"My Sweet Lord"...

Even now I get goose bumps, remembering this moment as I fell to my knees trying to make sense of it all. Hands cupped over my mouth, I sobbed with emotion.

Through my tear stained eyes I tried to focus on the image as the words were now visible across the TV screen. George Harrison had died and word was just breaking on the east coast. It was 5 a.m. in Boston on November 29. My husband appeared by my side and we stood there, holding each other for a very long time, in awe and disbelief at what had just happened...

. . .

I have come to believe that time is an illusion and 'all time' is really *'no time'* at all, so "what time" it was didn't really matter to me. My deep, inner soul self knew that I had just witnessed George's crossing and I was deeply moved and shaken beyond words. *(I have often wondered if we are of the same 'soul group' as we do share a similar family surname. I am also hope full that one day I will be able to share this experience with George's wife and family. I think they would be heart warmed to know that George went out blazing across the universe with a great big smile on his face!)*

There have been many nights and mornings that I have woken up from similar experiences but none as extraordinary or profound as this night had been. Oftentimes, I wake up speaking words out loud, some words that I have never even heard of before. Other times I just speak these words out loud without prompting. One of these words is "Hotehay". It would be several years before I would learn its meaning. For this reason, I keep my journal next to my bed so I can write them down as soon as I get up for I know the significance will unveil itself in good time. I also know if I don't write it down right away, it soon gets lost in the busy-ness of my day.

Much of this poetry is inspired from my dreams. Real, imagined or otherwise, dreams are our spiritual reflections and experiences from the other side. That is why journaling is such a great way to learn more about ourselves and is a very powerful tool on the path to healing and spiritual growth!

Spirit food for thought: *Wake up and dream!*

May you be blessed and inspired on your own soul journey to take a deeper look at the world that surrounds you. *Both waking and in dreamtime...*

Hotehay! *(Lakota: move over, Spirit's coming in!)*

Spirit

- ~ *Fairy Dream*
- ~ *Soulstice 21*
- ~ *Art Conjecture*
- ~ *Premier Grande Cru*
- ~ *GODWEB*
- ~ *Zodiac*
- ~ *Quantum Query*
- ~ *Spirit Guides Breath*
- ~ *Buddha Full*
- ~ *Wickiup*
- ~ *Crossing Guard*
- ~ *Akin of Ten*
- ~ *Helixir of the Gods*
- ~ *Troubadour*
- ~ *Gypsy Folk*
- ~ *Transplantformation*
- ~ *Forge On*
- ~ *Reason*
- ~ *O'Seeker*
- ~ *Yosef*

Why are we here? What is our purpose? Perhaps we should go to sleep to find the answer!

I have learned a lot about myself since I started keeping a dream journal. I believe that our dreams hold the solutions to our waking life problems and quite possibly the keys and symbols to unlock our very life's purpose.

But before we go about solving the mysteries of our lives we must first believe this to be true; only then will we be open to receive the messages that lie within.

What once was a great pastime has now become just that—a time of the past. Naps! Why don't people take naps anymore? If time is an illusion then why do we keep saying "there's just no time"?

Day dreaming is such a wonderful avenue to help develop the creative side of our nature. Is there anything more inviting than napping in a hammock on a warm summer afternoon?

Feel the light breeze gently brushing up against your face, encouraging you to let go, dream on, and journey off into that fantasy land which beckons in the distance...

One day while I was complaining about never seeming to get a particular chore done, my wise beyond her years, then 22 year old daughter Jesse said something to me that I will never forget. She said "Mom, you shouldn't always focus on your ends or you will never enjoy your means".

She stopped me in my tracks that day and I have never looked back.

Life truly IS a journey; not a destination. So take time out of your day whenever possible to take a nap or daydream a little. While creating our own little fantasy world we give ourselves a much needed rest by slowing down and being still.

And who knows? If you're lucky, the dream you catch along the way may just be what the doctor ordered...

"...to sleep, perchance to dream!" ~Shakespeare

Fairy Dream

1-5-2006

How still the night when you're not there
Across the sky far away from here
Fly off into the sunset of clouds
Whispers are heard, but no, not aloud

Fairy dream catcher
Fly o'er my night
Protect sacred thoughts
Hold fast, keep them tight

I wonder in bliss, I wander in love
Imagine your kiss, your face just above

How captive the voice wheneth speak from afar
How familiar the song once heard on a star
Reclaim my soul and remember the day
We said fear not love, for love finds a way

Oh fairy dream catcher
Fly o'er my night
'Tis time to surrender
Our love to the light

The mist, it sits, on the water and waits
As if someone else were deciding its fate
A lilting, lingering fragrance of thee
Arouses my soul ~ how it doth set me free

My prayers, meditations and incense they burn
My soul longs to capture what my spirit so yearns

Oh surrender the dream
Fairy catcher to me
The essence of yesterday
Of what is to be

How soft the sun as it glistens on high
Atop salty froths, water fairies sigh

Fairy dream catcher, fly back o'er the night
When we welcomed the dream of our starry twilight
For time it means nothing, it's fluid you see
One great and cosmic transiting sea

I dream catch the fairy
And fly back to my space
Where she fills me with love
Fills me with grace
This gold dusting reverence and remembrance of thee
Is dream catching freedom; *it's what sets me free...*

Someday I'll go back there—back to a place that I've never been and never left.

The place high atop rocks overlooking the sea—but what sea?

Where the wind calls to me and tousles my hair, whispers names, friends...yes, of course, my olde friends!

Such a fond remembrance ~ in the deep secret places of my soul...

I wrote this on the summer solstice—perhaps the portals were open that day and took me back there so easily...

Like shadows and light reflections bouncing images off trees, silhouettes- they are there, they are all still there. As am I. And one day soon I will visit there again; perhaps next summer solstice the way will open up for me once more, only this time bringing me all the way there.

Back, into the shadows, and reflections, of my olde self.

"Man is a spiritual being—a soul, in other words—and that this soul takes on different bodies from life to life on earth in order to at last arrive at such perfect knowledge, through repeated experience, is to enable one to assume a body fit to be the dwelling place of a Mahatma or perfected soul. Then, they say, that particular soul becomes a spiritual helper to mankind".
~ H.P. Blavatsky

Soulstice 21

{*A maze in Grace*}
6-21-2006

Spirit balm
to salve the wounds
of the soul and mind
Body
Physical solutions
To a soul evolution
Reality illusion

Wounded heels of time
Come round and round again
Fly off to reign
In the sunsetting wind
Circles and wheels
Sanskritten forever
Ever is a very long time
To wither
So salve up the wounds
And save the soul
For it longs
Soul longs

Free
Peace and free with thee
Is love again to be
Beegotten of hives
And nothing beyond nothingness
Empty the chalice

Only to fill it again
With the light
Womb men of the Light
Siri Mirah
Her reflection in space
Originates only in GOD's divine grace

Surrender to me
Serenity
Alone in the woods
Of groves and roots
Sweet destiny I'n thee
In shady palms and secret places
Of hiding
Soul hides amidst the shade
Allowing the sun only a peek
Oh speak
To me now
Here there
You go again
Fly fire fly

An elixir arises
It cultivates pearls
Recycled in dreams
Old yarn tales and earls
Tie up these threads
Of the wisdom and drink
I wait at the well
Of deep inner peace
Deep subjects inter
Ring subjects and myrrh
Immersion subversion
Collect at the stem
Send it surrend it
Harken the shem

Shekinah
Rosinah
A Reginald
Ahem
Amen is to thee
Amenti of me

So be it
Speak to it
Speak of it and through
It finds and it winds all the way
Back to you

Fluids of Druids
Snippets of tine
Tuning up universal
Harmony of mind
Wings and rings and tubular bells
Protecting the signs
show the way
YAHWEH foretells

In synaps of space
In gaps of the brine
Aloft in the waves
Afloat in the mine
Awaken an'stirs
Allah maids of the mist
Rock continents of eyes
Are you getting the gist

See all two behold
And hold two the bee
Sun lengthened days
Enlightening chi
As if glowing thru honey

Sweet reflections agree
That this soul-sticing journey
Brings moon gold for thee...

When I used to work in Boston, each morning always held a visual treat for me. After arriving at Long Wharf via the commuter boat, I would walk up State Street or through Quincy Market, past Government Center towards my office building. No matter which way I went, my gaze was always drawn upwards to take in the incredible architecture of olde that never ceased to amaze me, capture my attention, arouse my curiosity...

For here, nestled in between skyscrapers of the 20th century, sit intricately carved stone buildings—*some more than 200 years old!*

Flowers, baskets of fruit, symbols, geometric shapes, lions, unicorns...

What do they all mean?

Why were these particular stone carvings etched into these buildings?

Who decided that??

I get the faint sense that I arouse their curiosity in me just as much.

I wonder...just as diamonds set in stone represent an intention of marriage ~ what do you suppose these stone sculptures and images hope to engage in us?

If only in the caverns of my mind, these stones speak...

Art Conjecture

Who speaks the language of the stones
So carefully carved up high
Who are those chosen faces
Who grace us in the sky

A gentle rose a lions face
A unicorn perched above
A horn a plenty basket of fruit
All etched in stone with love

Some shields emblazoned with emblems
Some left blank for you and me
To wonder what they all might mean
A message destined for us to see

Such beautiful intricate designs
All customary and free
To surpass the weathering storms
That drug most out to sea

Forein the brick and mortar
A muse still hears those words
That ladled out the mention
And directed the flags unfurled

You know most they never notice
Never look inside to see
Even when it's plain as day
They cannot waste their energy

This all is good for it's not for all
But for some instead it's real
As it tells a story ne'er ever told
And many along route have felled
The story you see is older than time
And the stones now ready to speak
And if you listen with your heart and soul
T'may bring a smile towards your cheek...

...Wish I may wish I might
Get the wish I wish tonight...

What if you had the opportunity to meet one famous person ~ who would it be?

I have been wishing to meet the same famous person for a long time now. He never ceases to impress me no matter what movie I see him in *(yes, he is an actor)*.

I fall out in laughter every time I watch him on Saturday Night Live *(no, he is not a regular but he has hosted)*.

There are certain words particular to his skits on that show and my husband and I can never say one of these words without ad-libbing his *accent...*

He can be both serious and hysterically funny all at the same time.

He is truly a transcendental actor who is recycled from another time and obviously *not* from this planet.

Ahhh...the robins would be singing as we go a'walkin' ~ on our way to a continental breakfast where we might share in some champagne...

Can you figure out who he is???

ok, if you can't stand it.... Here is the mirror image...
neklaw rehpotsirhc

Premier Grande Cru

Take a walk in the vineyard of consciousness
Drink of their virtual wine
Taste their ancestral passionate fruit
Serving the collective cup of their minds

Wander on thru their fields lined with grapes
Pick from their overhead hang
How sweet the taste of their mulberry bush
Their champagne reverie drives you insane

Passages in time from so long ago
Written the unspoken word
Makes their debut amidst puzzles and plain
In sight almost seems so absurd

Old is now now is here rest assured

The beech trees wisdom not found on the beach
Nor lined in the vineyards of home
Yet they speak in the groves by the way of the loaves
In messages digested by you
From cups serve a most golden hue
If your will to surrender comes due

Wood is the paper and paper the tree
Arcane the knowledge for few
Recycled the way so the messages stay
They light up this humorous view
With writing utensils so few
A papyrus and bloodwort will do

A meal is complete it's counterpart too
When appetites whet once again
And drink in the wealth of the family vine
Preserved as a Premier Grande Cru

On parchment a note and primitive pen
This menu writes out just for you
The table that waits at heavenly gates
Now set to serve wine up for two

A consecration at best for one who behest
Sounds a perfect and singular HU
For the wine of the time sings the song of the vine
Now your voice will keep singing it too...

Everything is connected.

Buddha has been telling us for thousands of years that there is no separate self.

We all emanate from the same Divine Source. Even though we all get to forge our own path, we are all ultimately heading towards the same goal of spiritual enlightenment, unity with the Great Divine, however or whatever we perceive that to be, it is just many paths back to the **ONE.**

So, there is nothing to fight over. No prize to win.

Mankind would benefit to listen to the wisdom of *Chief Seattle* who tells us:

"Man did not weave the web of life; he is merely a strand in it. Whatever he does to the web, he does to himself."

I imagine **GOD** has had enough, and wonder if he is asking "Please?"

Please...plea...ease...see...peace...please...

GODWEB

4-15-2007

Spirit lines that cross
Letters that disappear
Illuminate the path
And lead us right back here

We started out at the beginning
Here at the very end
To reconcile our basic truths
With the signs we've asked to send

This spider web of light
Is weaving a divine path
A sum of gematric equations
In a course of sacred math

Wisdom of the ancients
Hidden messages for us to see
Redeem them now they cry to us
To fulfill life's destiny

Accept the things we do not know
For they help to weight the ground
Move from the place that speaks to us
In prayer, love, music and sound

Forein there lies a great secret
GOD's most amazing grace
Wake up to see her reflection
Mirrored back upon your face

Echoed moments here and there
Absorbed across the land
Deep the roots soaked in sweat
Their toils uphold the plan

When thresholds open doors unseen
Please close your eyes to see
The answers have always been within
Only your truth will set you free

GOD's web of light is gossamer silk
With wings of silver and gold
Thru shooting stars and heavenly pearls
Spider way of light it unfolds…

Astrology is a funny thing; either you believe it or you don't. It's alot like the tarot cards, folks either seek their wisdom or they shy away from it all together.

I was drawn to both in my teenage years, but then my religious upbringing over-shadowed things like that as "dark" so I surrendered my interest out of fear.

Nowadays, I surrender my fear out of interest!

I have detached from the religious dogma of my youth and am finding great joy and freedom in the spiritual expression of a universal way to be— LOVE.

I am fascinated by the cosmos. Astrology is really just an earthly map of the universe—our galaxy, so to speak. To have your birth chart done is to take a snapshot of how the universe looked the very moment you entered into existence. I would imagine this to have a huge impact on how we grow and develop, mentally and spiritually over the years. When you consider the particular attributes of each planet along with the specific characteristics of each zodiac sign, you begin to get a pretty good sense of an individual's unique personality traits. As the world turns and planets move in and out of each of the 12 signs, they paint a certain picture overall influencing the day.

Hence, the horoscope.

And there is so much more to the zodiac than newspaper horoscopes— but like anything worth knowing, we have to uncover this truth on our own...

Zodiac

(for Massa Phat)

In the house of humans
I sit sipping tea
Such an interesting view
I could just let it be
But I ponder my journey
My way out the door
For I know it will lead me
The place I yearn for

I see it I want it I know it exists
The freedom I envision
The path paved with bliss
So I unravel to travel
This way it must be
You must want out
Must want to be free…

Enter into the lodge of spiritual kin
Begin to expand your knowledge within
Visit all their houses each one their own gift
A transiting byzantine celestial lift

The ram she makes way to get your foot out the door
But the first step you must take—you have to want more
Constellation the bull helps you connect
Holds your hands in the ethers, spiritual hug 'round your neck
Nothing can stop Gemini's twins by your side
Both paths they will take you, illusions override

Some they will wonder if you're being led astray
But the crab she knows why you must walk your own way

The lion is lovely and rests well in his den
A deep breath sets up his settling in
The virgin she smiles as she begins to let go
Transcending the physical, she flows with the know
Balance and justice come thru loud and clear
When you tune the universal harmonies of your mind's atmo-
    sphere
The scorpion she blazes her fiery path
Illumes with her heart, there's no turning back
Sagittarius the healer helps release, remove blocks
When you empty the vessel, new opportunities knock

Billy goats abound recycling swill
Refreshed and renewed the spirit refills
And practice makes perfect, water baptizes the wise
A query of adepts, acute awareness, no surprise
Pisces the fish, water divinity of olde
Brotherhood of the Buddha's ancient wisdom unfolds...

Good thing I paid attention to the drumbeat of my soul
For if I held myself captive these things I'd not know

Won't you please come and join me a nice cup of tea
Savor a dip in the zodiac sea
Forein the 12 house are gifts meant for thee
O'knowledgeable wind, fill my sails, set me free~

I don't have a Masters Degree or a PHD…but I do have a very curious mind. That coupled with my Virgo nature, I suppose one could pen me a degree of inquisitive and logical with an insatiable thirst for knowledge.

I am also an energy healer. I so enjoy working with the subtle energies of the body helping myself and others learn to balance the mind, body and spirit.

These quantum physical particles of nature have science and holistic folks all paying attention these days.

If you've ever read anything about quantum physics, you would have to agree that it entails a language all unto itself. While reading up on it one day, the words stymied me; yet at the same time I knew exactly what they were talking about. *What's up with that?*

It moved me to poetic jargon, a verbiage of who knows what.

Since life is my educator, I guess I will just have to wait for the grade to come back on this one.

I feel like my answers are correct—but somehow, *I missed the question…*

Quantum Query

Exotic baryons flavoring charm
Celestial navigation barometric alarm
Density of fluids anti matter of space
Ephemeris your daily ground back into place

Nadirs and zeniths epochs of time
During hours of twilight
Heliocentrics align
Free flowing fluids
Form the density of quartz
Light emissaries mechanic
And navigational charts

Variables of symmetry
Integral physics a trace
Cross staff and back staff
Of Jacob's embrace

Meridians and latitudes
Directions in line
Imaginary stirrings and strings without rhyme
A compass to lead you intercepting when most
Follow theories thru the vortex
Spacing vectors of ghosts

Terminal velocity can only be reached
In critical dimensions if physically unbreached
Photons and gamma rays holographic clues
Profiles the question
And azimuth
of
you...

Once while on a Sylvia Browne cruise, I had the opportunity to sit in audience with her. If you were lucky and your ticket number was called, you got to stand up and ask her one question. People were asking everything from personal issues to the whereabouts of long lost loved ones.

When my number got called, I stood up knowing exactly what I would ask her. "What is my spirit guides name?"

She didn't even flinch and before looking away to the next person she said just one word to me ~ "Teddy".

We all have them you know. Our own personal angels, spirit guides. You may not be conscious of it, but they whisper wisdom in our ears and work wonders in our lives. Imagine what would happen if we WERE conscious of it!

Praying to me is not about saying 10 Hail Mary's or 3 Our Father's…it is speaking to our CREATOR and the angels in an honest and earnest fashion. I have always done this, ever since I was little.

But how will we ever benefit from their guidance if we don't first invite them into our lives and ask for their help?

Be still, go within…and believe that they exist. Ask for an unmistakable sign and be open to receive knowing it can come in many ways. Remember that GOD works in mysterious ways—so if you are only looking to the sky for a hand held sign you will surely miss the wisdom of the redbird sitting at your bird feeder or remember the images from your dreams or see the signs as messages along the road while driving, perhaps on a bumper sticker or maybe even written across a billboard along the highway.

Nature alone sends us hundreds of messages every day! And there are countless books and websites on animal wisdom and dream interpretation.

Dare to believe! What do you have to lose, *other than your mind…*

Spirit Guides Breath

1-6-2006

A fresh blanket of snow
A dazzling sunset
The warm summer breeze
Might it all bring you comfort

The redbird calls back
Your childhood of joy
Such a wild and untamed
Lightening sparked boy

Spirit of the Wind
Watch over you now
Hold fast for in time
The way shows you how

The river still calls
The way of the wild
Come hold me close
It's alright my child

Let the voices all speak
Each one their own turn
It allows for release
Of this you must yearn

Spirit of the Night
Hold you close in your sleep
Peace and love lullabies
And counting of sheep

The Shamans Lodge sweat
Will cleanse toxins and purge
Before long you'll see
The new you emerge

Remind of the day
Ye'll not let me be
My intentions of Love
Wish to just set you free
Spirit of the Sky
Fly with you tonight
Sleep well my friend
'til morning, *goodnight.*

I think my own personal "soul journeying" began when a friend introduced me to the teachings of the Buddha. I fell in love and soon became totally immersed in the thoughts, the ideas, *the way...*

Learning to close my eyes to see and become a "witness" to myself was a new concept for me as it is for most of us Westerners.

We are all spirits having a physical experience ~ not physical beings have a spiritual experience.

If we would just slow down, quiet our minds, take a break and come unplugged from the 21st century world of technology, we would give our energy field a much needed rest!

We are not our bodies. We are not our minds. And deceptive intelligence hits the road when the Buddha shows up.

True peace of mind is just the blink of an eye away. Try it!
Close your eyes, be still, go within. If only for a few minutes a day, we will change the way we view the world, ourselves. It cannot possibly be seen when our eyes and ears are affixed to cell phones, video games, computers, television, radios, headsets, laptops....

Why not treat yourself to a Buddha full morning, afternoon or evening~!

Allow yourself to enter into the silence of the stillness in the deepest secret places of your mind, your soul.

For in the silence of this stillness, *everything becomes clear.*

"You cannot travel the path until you become the path itself"
Buddha

Buddha Full

It's a Buddha full thing
learning to witness the mind
to step out of our madness
and sanity find

A wealth of conclusion
derivative zest
leave behind the illusion
give ourselves a real rest

Buddha smiles for a reason
he goes inside to see
and if you close your eyes
you will most amazingly agree

We are not the sum of our body parts
though most days we feel their worth
we are intricate facets of our spiriting self
who's purpose so waits to give birth

So when life begins to get you down
it's just a game, commit not to play
instead, be still, and go inside
witness yourself and drift away

We enlighten the mind when we unweight the body
so let your spirit self be light
see thru all the smoke and mirrors
give your soul the freedom of flight

And give thanks today for this Buddha full thing
of tapping into the source of our own power
then witness the way for our spirits foray
into a soul searching wilderness hour....

Do you wake up at night? Is it usually around the same time?

Do you ever wake up and think *'wow, what a crazy dream'!?*

Even though our bodies are sleeping in the wee hours, our spirits and resting minds are still busy working in harmony trying to help us find answers to our life situations.

When I started paying attention to what time I was waking up and started writing down my dreams, I was amazed at the amount of detail that was coming through.

Try it sometime!

Jot down those crazy snippets of dreams before they fade away and then ponder them for a day or two. Symbols, images, pictures, people, animals, numbers...they really do all mean something. If we are looking for answers to our every day dilemmas, sometimes all we have to do is ask.

Here's a simple exercise you might wish to try...as you lay yourself down to sleep each night, ask your higher source for guidance or direction with whatever is on your mind. Then take note of your dreams, crazy as they may seem, for in time, they may very well lead you to the answer. Be sure to keep a pen and paper nearby so you can write everything down before they get lost in waking hours.

Who knows? Maybe our mind is the *only* thing getting in the way...

Wickiup

Wolf comes to me in my dreams
Reminds me of things long not seen
I follow him back up into the hills
Alone, God's peace instills

I look around, take in the lay of the land
The peace and the quiet help me understand
My connection, relation, my deep earthen roots
The meaning behind Kokopelli's distant flutes

I arrive at a place prepared just for me
Under the stars near the juniper tree
Collect some fat wood start a warming fire
Wolf sits close by, his watch likens desire

Rubbing old sticks the coal starts to build
I am about spent when a spark finally yields
Placed upright in a bird nest of debris
Blow gently 'til the fire takes his first breath from me

I lean back and relax, savoring this view
Wolf now horizontal, seemingly mesmerized too
I can read from his eyes as the silence instills
The importance of our meeting in these heavenly hills

My eyes close to dream and see the wickiup in place
Lodge of the olde ones, their abode I now grace
I am sitting with many round a river bed of rocks
I listen intently while the elders each talk

You've spoken your voice says the phoenix who brings
Healing to my throat as my soul rises and sings
I chant out a dirge, my ancient soul song
It must originate from the place that my soul still belongs

With a deep breath and sigh, tears roll down my cheek
I turn to the faces offering words I can't speak
They have dusted my soul energies back into place
I am cleansed, I am safe, in their sacred embrace

As smoke rise up, embers burn deep within
Each breath I let go removes scarring and sin
The reflection is clear as they tend to remind
All is revealed, in Indian time

My puha returns, my minds eye revolves
I soak up the clarity of my mysteries solved
I bow my head in deep reverent thanks
And lend one last look at my memories banks

'Tis been a long road traveled most of my life
Stumbled many a block endured many a strife
In the blink of an eye it can all come undone
How I've prayed for this day, my soul shine in the sun

I wake in the morning to the call of the crow
Notice the warmth of my blanket is really lobo
Asleep on the ground with me safe by his side
To protect whilst I travel with my spiritual guide

As we wander on back down the hillside so green
Parallel in the traces, my wolf friend serene
He almost smiles to acknowledge this journeys end
And a new one beginning, just 'round the bend

I am blessed to be guided and protected this way
I commune with my angels and give thanks every day
I get lost in my thoughts, in the wickiup of my dreams
Until the alarm clock goes off, and I wake up
~ *or so it seems...*

I suppose we don't remember these things for a reason.
Yet human as we are, we often wish we could.

Protection of the soul is a precious commodity.
Our brains would surely get in the way and disturb our karmic destiny if it had all the pieces to our puzzle up front...

Trust in the way as it is set before us.

For the intricate nature of the human being is eternal at best...
no matter what we think...

"You would know the hidden realm where all souls dwell.
The journey's way lies through death's misty fell.
Within this timeless passage, a guiding light does dance.
Lost from conscious memory but visible in trance."

~Michael Newton ("Journey of Souls")

Crossing Guard

6-17-2007

Oh to the stars I long to flee
Across the sky to eternity
A passage thru time on the wings of a dove
Thru great cosmic dust in the name of Love

Swirls in my dreams in front of my eyes
Wondering what lies on the other side
An open expanse of silver and gold
Amidst shimmers of stars the galaxy unfolds

Of dust we are and to dust shall we return
To my own swirling mass one day I'll sojourn
But for now 'tis fine sitting guard at the gate
Showing others the way on their destiny's date

A thought, an imprint, psychic image in the sky
This place we return to without a question of why
Knowing peace and harmony within the ONE
Affirms our journey has just begun

This great cosmic swirl etched in time holding space
A recognition of sorts without seeing a face
Crossing guard looks around before opening the way
As the soul group reclaims their singular stray

Then returns to her post to await the next cross
Ensuring none lose their way none get lost
For the burning and yearning of home fills her days
And the swirls in her eyes never cease to amaze....

I have always heard other music within music. Sampling, I think they call it in the business. Likewise with words, I see other words within words. All things arrive in many layers for me so it's true when they say 'nothing is really what it seems'.

Language has always fascinated me and I love to play on words as certain 'roots' bump in and out of each and every dialect; easy to pick up if you know a few basics of language and begin to see their patterns.

Many people, including myself, have been fascinated with the ancient history of Egypt along with its pharaohs and queens. This poem was inspired by a certain Egyptian pharaoh of the 18th dynasty who lived mid 1300 BC.

Much has been written about him and his wife, Nefertiti over the years. Many have commented on his flawless knowledge of the solar system and of this royal couples marked influence on monotheism.

His name, Akhenaten, translates to mean "effective spirit of Aten"—"Aten" being attributed to the solar disc of the sun. Akhenaten is also believed to have composed a "Great Hymn to the Aten"; a poetic piece which some believe to be repeated in one of the biblical books of the Psalms.

So, perhaps words really do go around and come around much more than we think. Maybe it's just a matter of remembering the original alphabet...

Akin of Ten

(Inspired by the 18th Dynasty)

Keeper keep pure
Hieroglyphics and dates
The keys to the kingdom
She waits at the gates

Your name it is written
So many different ways
The kinship conclusive
Evidence admitted now stays

Master of horses
Charioteer of olde
Confidante of the king
Wise companion worth his gold

Partners from the beginning
Of time can never tell
The distance not measured in numbers
Biblical books of Heaven and hell

Bound together in time
Through out all eternity
Pieces come back together
Unveiling sacred mysteries

Tapestries and tenets, a modicum of prose
Why to sing these songs of old, heaven only knows
Sweet sounding melodies grazing in the grass
Deliverance of the angel's words, spoken from the past

Temperate times now revealing the way
Caught between the mystic and magical array
Opens up a channel not seen until now
For the road less traveled is tacking at the bow

Side by side in tombs of dust
Twin robes that bind still keep sacred trust
Now begin to stir from the longest sleep
Reclamation for the queen—*no more shall she weep...*

I am a Virgo. I seek. I search. And I re-search some more.

Our minds have such infinite possibility and we should never stop learning, never stop searching...for the truth, for our truth.

Knowledge is key and I want to know everything!

The double helix has long been a symbol of eternity, transformation....

"Helixir" is my play on two words...'helix', relating to a 3 dimensional upward rising spiral and 'elixir', an alchemic preparation or essential principle quite possibly found in the fountain of youth.

Is this the alchemic essence of true love?

Could this be what the Medieval Grail Romances and Troubadours of the time were writing and singing about?

What did the alchemists of the Middle Ages *really* know?

To reach that place, that endless, timeless, spiritual place....
To transform and advance into higher realms of being...
To be fully and freely out of our body, and out of our mind...
Crossing time and space and all boundaries of the mind....

Ah, this so stirs my spine!

If we are all images of our Creator, of GOD, then I am a GODDESS... projecting Goddessence...I raise my chalice and invite you to drink with me, the Helixir of the Gods...and hopefully you too, will soon be, out of your body, *and right out of your mind...*

Helixir of the Gods

4-24-2007

Serpentine the spinal tap
Arising up within my lap
Chaste the touch who's cosmic spark
Begins the elixir's sacred march

Light years apart yet hand in hand
A magnetic meld of woman and man
Surrender to ride the spiney beast
A sumptuous sensuous passion feast

Leaving the lodge one breaks a sweat
Time stands still when appetites whet
A breathy sighing expulsion of sound
Imaginings for thee from the Venus mound

Transference of time, energy, space
Helix unravel your lips about face
Spinning the sanskritten wheels of time

Out of my body
Out of my mind

Spurts of the spirit push up thru the crest
Expelling sweet particles of sensual zest
Most exquisitely aroused by the essence of thee
Volumes not spoken of words set me free

Soul mates and cell mates entangled in moss
Travel the channel of lines that still cross
To share in the ecstasy music of sound
Cosmic twins once lost are now both found

Ardent the spirit at twilight and dusk
Translucent the lover's scentsational musk
Ascending and bending the helix' array
This climax unravels a Great Milky Way

Helixir of the Gods that so stirs my spine
Awakens Goddessence, my channel divine
A galactic orgasm of words hard to find

Send me out of my body
And right out of my mind...

If music is the language of the spirit then we are all musicians.

Sound is vibration and vibration is healing.

Does that make all musicians healers?

By allowing the healing opportunities that present to us at various stages (on various stages) of our lives, we open ourselves up to a higher resonance of balance.

There is so much more to healing than a trip to the Dr.'s office. Think about when we scrape or bump ourselves, what is our instinctive reaction? We touch it! Maybe our instincts to touch is not only about comfort.

Energy follows thought and thought follows intention.

There are many musicians who use the stage as a powerful tool to express much more than the sheer entertainment of their music and words. All we have to do is be open to the possibility in order to participate in that intended action.

Think about your favorite piece of music—see if you can uncover the granules of sand and stone that make up the magical moments that speak to you each time. Listen not with your ears, but with your very being ~ your breath.

There is so much more to be found when we silence the mind, and listen ~ to the spaces between the music...

"Find the way, not the way out"
Grace Walsh

Troubadour

Mosaic of minds
Messianic at best
In sanity of dreams
Thoughts and arrows suggest

Soufflés across time
Elemental ingredients attest
Myriads of mirrors
Royal reflections in jest

Monarchs and mummies
Viceroys and men
Coins that pay ladies
Remind me of when

Our mavericks were silenced
No speaking their truth
Headbands bore diamonds
Diadems of Ruth

Time less travel
Aesir ring in space
Your visage escapes me
Yet I recognize your face

Disappearing ink
From antiquities well
A faint remembrance
Of recognition tells

So many flavors
Taste tempt me each time
As I reconcile the morsels
Of indigenous rhyme

Though the way is still veiled
Strumming citterns remind
Of once passionate buskers
Who's performance in line

Souls questing for truth
Requesting their sign
Not a key left unturned
'til their lyrics found mine

For the nature of nature
Of what's natural at best
Are the rhythym's of timbrels
Intoning us, *lest…*

Did you ever wonder where the tarot cards originated?

As a kid growing up, there were certain stigmas attached to anything of that nature. Out of fear, I stayed away from those kinds of things during those years.

But what if they were created to help us?
To leave a trail or to pave a particular path...

Could they have been a road map of higher guidance and wisdom??

What if the images represented messages that had to find a way to carry through the ages? What if they had to survive under the most scrutinizing of eyes??

Did you ever wonder if or how every day playing cards and tarot cards relate to each other?

Perhaps the elders of long ago knew they had to find a way to preserve certain messages and these cards presented the perfect way to get those messages out to the four corners of the Earth.

The wandering gypsies of olde would have been the perfect folk to spread these messages. And perhaps the elders knew, those who were pure of heart and without fear would recognize the messages embedded deep within these printed cards. Those open to receive these messages would gain insight on the deeper meanings of life, nature and how to walk in balance.

Today, this original deck has multiplied with each new interpretation and people, translating into all languages and cultures.

There are countless decks, each with their own passionate imagery; but just as in the days of olde, one need not speak a particular language to interpret these cards...for the *truth speaks loud without uttering a word...*

Gypsy Folk

The King of Hearts lights up the night
His love stretches across the lands
His Queen a love unto herself
Her Knight she'd rather hold hands...

The King of Clubs beats on his chest
No heart inside to bruise
His Queen her power more important
And power they did abuse...

The King of Diamonds shines brightest of all
His Queen most brilliant too
Imparting wisdom and fairness of law
Royal lineage of the privileged few...

King of Spades most wicked and mean
You dare not disagree
No questions asked when he silenced his Queen
No chance to ever be free...

Fortune tellers they roamed the land
Delivering hope and warnings too
Imprinted images only they'd understand
Their cards spelled it out just for you...

Of such a dangerous treacherous roue
They desperately tried to leave clues...

And games of **Poker** of merry folk
Who's heads lined up in suits

They tell a story of many who died
Designating those in evil cahoots

G*in* **R***ummy* is found with seven of a kind
But not so kind in truth
Sin rummy is more the name of the game
When drunken their deals so uncouth

What were they really *F*ishing for
Looking each for their own kind
The fish a metaphor for *Christ*
Only their *Savior* could break this bind
No wonder they turned to *Solitaire*
Less trouble when all alone
But then again it would always depend
Which King sat on the throne...

...John also came forward, he said : " O Lord, command me also that I say the interpretation of the words which thy light-power once prophesized through David." But Jesus answered and said to John: "Thou also, John, I command thee to say the interpretation which my light-power prophesized through David.:

10. " Mercy and truth have met one another, and righteousness and peace has kissed one another."
11." Truth has sprouted from the earth and righteousness has looked forth from heaven."

John answered, however, and said : "This is the word which thou hast said to us once : " I came forth from the height, I entered into Sabaoth the Good , I embraced the light-power within him.".... " Mercy and truth have met one another."....." Righteousness is thou who didst bring all the mysteries through the Father, the First Mystery who looks within, and thou didst baptise the power of Sabaoth the Good . And: "Truth which has sprouted from the earth." . .. thou didst come down upon him who is Jesus our Saviour, like a dove....

...Now it happened when John had spoken these words, the First Mystery who looks forth said to him : "Excellent, John, thou beloved brother."...

Excerpted from Chapter 63
Pistis Sophia: Book Two

The teachings of Yeshua/Jesus were purely spiritual in nature, practiced by purely spiritual people known to some as the Essenes, Nazirenes (off shoots of David/keepers, followers of Jesus of Nazareth) and/or Ebionites (poor ones). It is said that these sacred teachings became impure when they were corrupted under the pagan roman rule of Constantine.

Forge On

7-15-2007

Searching for revelations
On land and sea and shore
A disclosure aforementioned
The message I am not sure

The words within the logos
Powers of the universe
Fundamental cosmos
No time left to rehearse

Bestowed by a deity
Animating vapors of thee
Infusion of the spirit
Sister syzygy

Associate elemental fire
To light revealing all
With identifying wisdom
To portals of grace on call

Charisma of the ancients
Encourage us to speak
Apocalyptic visions
Of John the Seer to seek

Universal Mother Sophia
Reveals perfect harmony
Blessed fruit upon her limbs
Obscured for centuries

Eagle Prophet of Patmos
Guide us with your vision
To choose the way of life or death
Our ultimate decision

Your name gets changed by many
Who suit you to their needs
But those of us still looking
Follow your spirit seeds

I wonder if you're watching
Lighting up our path with sun

I wonder if you're asking
Are you looking?

Forge on...

Did you ever notice how we succeed in getting those things that we <u>really</u> want? Be it a dress on sale, half the asking price at a yard sale or trying to get others to see our point of view...

Imagine if we were that relentless in ALL aspects of our lives.

If losing were *not* an option.

If <u>all</u> our experiences were peak experiences.

What kinds of seeds would we plant in the gardens of our mind then?

How would our spirits be transformed?

If we never experienced heartache would our love just keep on growing?

What do we really need?

Maybe the only thing we really "knead" has more to do with bread; *communion with GOD.*

"The transformation toward eternal life is gradual. The heavy gross energy of body, mind and spirit must first be purified and uplifted. When the energy ascends...then self mastery can be sought..."

~ Lao Tzu ("Hua Hu Ching":71)

Transplantformation

Special delivery
A heart arrives for thee
Words of the heartbeat
That the eyes cannot see

Calling to you now
They cry from afar
Love takes my hand
Sings me home to the star

Twinkles far
Twinkles near
Twinkles sighing in my ear

Reach up for the clouds
Grab hold and float past
Shapes found with your eyes
Now real at long last

Angel wings of a bird
Buddha's belly full of laughs
Rainbows edge takes you home
Amid angel herald staffs

Sparkles high
Sparkles low
Sparkles within let you know

You must fly without wings
You must walk off the ground

Angel songs you must sing
Such sweet fragrant sounds

But if wings become too heavy
And a hitch the only ride
Remember the strength of the mustard seed
Holding tiny miracles inside

For the road less traveled
Is full of stumbling blocks
But when turned into stepping stones
The way it soon unlocks

Expressions deep
Express afar
Expressing light beams off the star

We never really walk alone
Although at times it seems
Transplantformation of broken hearts
Helps reconcile dreams

Live from the spirit
Not your head

Express yourself out loud
The voices held so deep within
Are lifting off their shroud

To twinkle sparkle and express
Their iridescent beams
And another chance for hearts to beat
In the bloodline of broken dreams...

Raison D'etre ~ (French)
"Reason to be"

We all need a reason, to be.
To live, to exist…

Why then
When our reason
Disagrees with theirs
Do they put a cross in front of it
And call it

treason

"I die for speaking the language of the angels."
~ Jeanne D'Arc

Reason

Raison d'etre
S'il vous plait
Allons'y
It's right this way

A foreign land
Speaks from a far
In the distance shines
As if from a star

However the way
Be it black be it white
It beckons the day
Ne'er give up the fight

For the way of the proud
Is truly a few
Its rhythmic sound
Resonates with you

So pick up your pipe
Let the smoke lead the way
Guide you back thru the time
And back into today

The message it brings ~ on messengers wings
Affirmations abound ~ in circles of round
Follow arrows and rings ~ leave no stone unturned
Madonna she sings, else effigies burn~

If I were to ask you 'What is truth?' you might answer honesty, integrity, certainty, perfection, loyalty, supreme reality...

Supreme reality takes me back to GOD—
so might truth be the *original nature of things?*

If truth is the supreme and honest original nature of things, then I have to wonder ~ what truly *is* our original nature?

Three things cannot be long hidden:
the sun, the moon and the truth.
~Buddha

O'seeker

I'm searching for an answer
To a question I do not know
Something that was asked of me
Oh so long ago

Remembrance not forgotten
Locked in memory
A fate of faith unspoken
Catching up to me

This myriad of mirrors
Reflects divinest truth
One click of the aperture
Reveals the darkroom proof

Memories of a mummies mind
Impossible to trace
Fleeting thoughts of days gone by
Etched upon your face

Synchronize the rainbows walk
In stepping stones on water
Doesn't matter time or place
Spirit food for fodder

A resonance of simpler times
Sparkling dew drop eyes
Faces from the past appear
Cast shadows to the skies

Forever is a very long time
For an answer not to wait
Hand in hand we tow our line
Together seal our fate

For the road is rough
And filled with stones
But the stones they are the key
To the knowledge locked deep inside
And the sacred wealth of seed
A little water and a little sun
The flower starts to grow
Heaven's rose it blooms today
And the answer in the wind *doth blow...*

I often close my eyes to see.
And what I often see, is not what is before me.

Curious enough, I realize, that my real eyes show me things are not always what they seem...

Do they glimpse some other place, some other time?

Of what once was, or perhaps, of what *might be??*

Makes me wonder...

Do you think a butterfly realizes
when he closes his real eyes
that he used to be...
a caterpillar?

Yosef

6-18-2007

Your coat of many colours
still wrapped around me
protects me from the elyments
on the great and restless sea

Why did ye have to stay behind
myne heart it breaketh so
yet deep insyde I know the truth
that love f'yrever grows

Ye stood in lyght n'ow lay in peace
your heart so pure n'proud
n'my last full measyre of love f'r you
wraps white linen y'er face n'shroud

Tell me a gain why this must be
Oh Lord expand my mystard seed
forein my faith n'hope my dreams
I'll stay this path for I know it leads

Thy staff and rod they comfyrt me
in times my sad despair
and the circle remains unbryken
of this I'm well awayre

When the moon ryses in the house of the sun
and the sun ryses to meet the day
there ye'll be amidst mountains so high
in y'er rainbow coloured array

I too atop the greenest hills
m'hair flowing in the wynd
be waiting there f'reconcyle
my Yosef, *my spirit kin*...

Soul Retrieval

As a seamstress, I understand how the many pieces of a pattern must fit together just right in order to complete the desired outfit. As an energy healer, I also understand that the pieces of our 'existence' are not only found in the physical realm but in the spirit realm as well. Some times things just have to fall apart to be put back together in the way it was intended to be. Like a strained muscle at the massage therapist's office, she/he will invariably massage it to the point of pain in order to break down the old thereby allowing new blood and oxygen to flow into the muscles and surrounding tissue. Likewise, evident in many of my sewing projects when I sewed something backwards, oftentimes the only way to fix it was to completely undo it. So, when things fall apart, sometimes it is just a necessary nudge from spirit giving us yet another chance to make it better, right.

Reiki is much the same concept—we must be willing to break out of old patterns and habits if we wish to rebuild our lives anew. I think of it as the great plan or template, pattern, if you will, that shows us the highest expression of ourselves. During a reiki session, one is transported to a place of total peace and relaxation; a place where anything seems possible. In our waking minds, we begin to attach and become attached by the surrounding situations in our lives which get entangled with our perfectly balanced spirit form.

Recognizing that all these things are 'plugged in' to us is the first step in coming unplugged from that which does not originate with us nor serves us any good. But, in order to free ourselves from the entrapments that drain our energy we must first recognize how they got there and sometimes <u>unlearn</u> or let go of the dogmas that have created this unhealthy reality in the first place. Easier said than done! But, if we are willing to go through whatever it takes and set our intentions towards one of healing and growth, we will surely reap the benefits for the rest of our lives.

Something I read once talked about how our spirits use this incarnation as a workshop, one that is designed to help us complete our evolution. Our spirit dance is to find out what our bodies came here to do—that's the hard part. To linger in the shadows is a fear of walking your destined path. To recognize your medicine out on your shirt sleeve but never bring it inward is a sacred denial at best! I had always seen it but never recognized it as my own. To trust in the divine guidance seemingly all around you, is to move forward in faith, even if you have no idea how you will do it—there is something to be said for this kind of TRUST. Think for a minute about the word 'trust' through my heyoka eyes—there are crosses on each end holding you up and U R smack dab in the middle! The 'S' is there to mirror your transformation, like a snake, shedding its skin when it is time to grow. A blessed reminder that we are being divinely cared for, especially when we have faith, *trust*.

It's no secret that we are living in challenging times; also no secret that we are living in the times prophesized by our elders and the ancients. And, it is no coincidence that there are so many healing modalities available to support us these days, more so than ever before! My spirit self senses that we are all being threaded through the eye of the cosmic needle. I would have to wonder if the ones having the hardest time right now are the ones in need of more soul work. Sooner or later, spirit is going to call in your number! I have to believe based on my own experience(s) that SPIRIT is done with the nudging, it's now time for the push! And it's a BIG push! As more and more people tap into to these higher vibrations and recognize their spirit self in the mirror, the Earth is also reflecting this energetic shift. Now is the time to take what works and fine tune it and leave behind what holds us back, weighs us down. In doing so, we leave behind all that doesn't fit through the "eye" of our spiritual needle...the needle that is quite possibly re-weaving the reason us Human Beings were placed here on Earth to begin with...to create a perfectly divine tapestry.

For many years now, I have been peeling back the layers of my onion, do-ing my own soul work. Some 'enlightenment's' were easier to take than others during this time and others not so pleasant. Sometimes the hardest thing one can do is look themselves in the mirror. Yet the more I became a "witness" unto myself, the more I embraced these experiences for they have served me well. Whether or not I knew just how much at the time, each have helped me to clear and clean out anything and everything in my energy field that did not serve my highest good.

Once I had started this process, being able to witness myself from an energetic point of view became quite the interesting image. I thought about the crack in my voice and my efforts to "fix", what I thought was broken. I had my ideas about why soul pieces of my voice had left and were further compounded over the years whenever I withstood criticism about my voice and whether or not I could sing. It occurred to me that this gap would probably always exist in my throat chakra because these soul pieces had ejected themselves during these different situations in my life. *How can you heal a piece of yourself that is missing??* I guess I had not really thought about it before or maybe I was not ready for it but it soon became my focus…it was time for me to get a soul retrieval. I had learned how to do this for others in my shamanic training but I had not had one myself. The more I thought about it the more it made sense. How can I 'mend' a piece of me that is no longer there? No wonder my voice still cracks, there is a big old gap there! Until I return the piece (or the piece willingly returns to me) I imagine my voice will always sound this way.

I pondered this for a long time and finally came to the conclusion that it wasn't about my voice anymore but more about being 'whole' once again. I wanted to bring back my soul parts that were missing—I missed that feeling, like a treasure map finally leading you to the pot of gold. Maybe this was what I had been searching for all along. To reclaim what was rightfully mine.

I had been given a gift certificate for my birthday from my Reiki teacher for a shamanic healing session. Truth be told, I had mixed feelings about this as I was a shamanic healer myself. Always vigilant to look inside my 'onion' I decided to seek the deeper meaning and trust that this was meant to be. Ah, when ego gets in the way we get all kinds of messed up!! *(no wonder the last 2 letters of the word ego end in "go!")*

It came as no surprise when I finally booked the healing session that this woman too seemed so familiar. Her healing space was like climbing into the womb and reflections of my own feathers, rattles and drums lined various shelves and wall space in the room. I chuckled to myself when I remembered that riverboat cruise with Sylvia Browne and how after waiting in line to meet her and have her sign my book, I offered to give her a reiki session (we were on the boat cruise together for four days). She smiled and said "Oh honey, I'm a Reiki Master, too." My reply was "Yes, but even the healer needs healing!"

The Shamanic healing session was just what the Dr. ordered. *(Thank you, Pat!)*

We talked for awhile afterwards and she suggested I might want to have a soul retrieval. I told her that I had been thinking about it for some time and agreed the time was right. She offered to barter with me and I was honored when this reflection came my way and grateful that I had trusted and let the last tidbits of my ego transform in the crackling fireplace of her healing room.

I set the appt and marked the date on my calendar. Each day I would note the day and honor myself with a little prayer of gratitude, thanking me for all the work I had done for myself up until now and reaching out with open arms, hugging myself, ready to welcome back those lost pieces of me.

The day finally came and I got ready with calm anticipation and eager awareness that something really profound was about to happen.

As I arrived at her house, I thought about the significance of the day. It was a New Moon which is a great time for new beginnings and the planting of new seeds. Also, the moon was in the sign of Taurus, an Earth sign, which is very grounding and also ruled by Venus which just so happens to rule the neck and throat! Surely no coincidence, yet another divine arrow pointing the way with a profound affirmation from the universe that I had much cosmic support this day for my soul essence' return.

We talked for awhile before the session and then she led me through a guided meditation to meet one of my guides/angels. I was to ask a question and then wait for the answer. Once done, any uncertainties I may have had were blown into a small stick and then given to the fire for transformation thus removing them from my system, both inward and outward.

I am now lying down on the table with warm cloths wrapped around my feet and blankets over me. She gently places an eye cover over my eyes; I take a deep breath and commit to let go of all thinking and emotion—trying to only be in pure awareness of the process I am about to embark on. She sits at my head and is soon made aware from her guides that she is to go to my feet and work there for awhile first—not what she had intended but she follows the instinct of her guides. Reflexology has always captured my interest; to be able to 'massage' all of the internal organs of the body just by massaging certain spots on the feet is still something that I wish to learn.

I totally sink into the comfort of the padded table as she begins to rub warm oils into my feet, seemingly following lines of energy or meridians that somehow connect and make sense to me.

She introduces something smooth and warm to my feet, a wax-like orb that arouses a sensation of how it must feel when an embryo rubs its foot up against the embryonic sac.

There are no words to describe this sensation or feeling as I have never felt it before on this earthly plane but something in me remembers it well. I am transported back into my embryonic self; a teeny, tiny new speck of life and though my literal body and brain are not yet formed, I can still feel, see and sense everything around me! I have knowledge and pure intelligence of all that is and suddenly I know that I have just 'arrived' in the womb. I float in this awareness and suddenly I see my divine umbilical cord—a cord of light flowing outward from me, heavenward. I realize I am about to witness my real birth!

I follow the cord to its source and hear/see/sense the olde ones talking about my life to be and that it is time for me to go, time to be born. I sense resistance on my part, not wanting to go as they continue to talk about my life, the struggles and hardships I will encounter and how I will overcome them, to find my way and my way back. They note something important at age 54, when I will reconnect with this divine cord. There will be much for me to do after this happens. My resistance does not last long as I am soon being sucked down what looks like a vacuum of light, into my mother's womb and my new human form.

She continues to massage and work on my feet and though I don't experience the 'literal' re-birthing, I sense that I have been born. I am little, so cute and feeling more hands washing over me, rubbing my little feet. My adult self recognizes this as my first foot rub! Shortly after being born, they stamp my footprint with ink and then wash and rub it clean. I like this feeling of rubbing, it's grounding. It's like an affirmation, of saying "You are here!"—I cannot speak yet but they are affirming it. I feel loved and safe in these hands. Touch is pure love to a newborn and I am hearing myself say *"Keep rubbing my feet!!"*

When she flexes my toes down, I feel an opening (called Bubbling Spring meridian she tells me afterward)—like someone is bleeding the pipes, letting something out while letting new in. The sacred wood Palo Santo burns and I welcome the scent—though I had never known it before, it is olde and very familiar. I am in the South American jungle and I hear panther (jaguar?)—I wonder if it is her breathing/shapeshifting as I know she is at my feet yet I feel her close to my face.

In my minds eye, I see the white lights dancing again, as I used to before my George Harrison experience. It looks like a beautiful white birds wings, flapping gently and moving ever so gracefully. She is working at my heart. Something has been placed at my neck/heart? I continue to watch the light dance and all of a sudden I see it vacuumed into my chest, then more, I count, *one, two, three, four, five??* There may have been more but I have counted five. All beautiful, white energetic beings, pure energy...

I take a deep breath and know that they were my soul pieces coming back to me—I embrace the sensation, again having no words to compare this feeling to.

She is at my head, I feel a ping in my lower left pelvic area, not sure what that is, then a fuzzy, energy feeling in my head. I can see golden eyes staring at me, in my mind I ask if it will step back so I can see who/what it is, but it fades away. She places a Tibetan bowl on my chest and softly plays; followed by tuning forks, rattle and earth chimes. She checks several Chinese pulse points followed by dabs of oil on my wrists. She is done and tells me to be still for a few minutes while she gets water and then tells me to slowly wiggle and stretch, removing the eye cover. I share my impressions with her and start crying while describing my rebirth.

She tells me my bear was there from the beginning, very big and protective. She saw panther as well and said they both wanted to 'attend' but my bear won out. Many angels/guides were present in the room, in a circle holding hands. She shared messages about my work to come and a spiritual gift that was given to me during the retrieval.

I sit up and put my socks and shoes on while she spreads out her deck of angel cards. I pull one—it is the Archangel Michael; a wonder full affirmation and ending to my soul retrieval for sure.

. . .

As I drive home, I feel like I am looking through different eyes, I feel more "dense"—like I have more cells or something. Hard to describe but a feeling that "more" of me is looking out through the windows of my soul (eyes). It was and is an amazing experience. I notice colors are more vivid and I feel more "present" in my skin.

When I got home, I decided to take my bear skin and go in for a nice long nap; my bear and I. No more images of throwing him away as a child when he broke. We are now completely together again and ready for the next part of our journey.

Aho!

P.S.
(Passionate Spirit)

Many times I have written about the black hole, rabbit hole, the void that is seemingly created when we lose a piece of ourselves for whatever reason in life. It makes sense now to me, that these voids get created when our soul pieces eject. No wonder we keep getting 'stuck' on certain memories and experiences that were not so pleasant for us. We have all "fallen in" to experiences like these from our past and it's a literal climb up and out to move beyond them. I see now that having a soul retrieval plugs up those holes for good!

Some time has passed now since my soul retrieval. I sill have the sensation that "more" of me is looking out through my eyes. A welcome feeling for sure! People have asked me if the reason or trauma memory associated with the soul loss also comes back when a soul retrieval is done. It does not. When your soul pieces are retrieved, the reason they left is left behind. This is where and how the true healing happens. There may be a memory floating around outside of you for a few moments, here or there; if this happens, think of it as that memory passing you by one last time as it floats away forever. It is not showing up to move back in—it cannot. The soul piece has sealed up that rabbit hole forever.

I have noticed a few thoughts associated with different experiences in my life come to mind these past few months; but it's different. They seem to exist "outside" of me now; there is no emotional/physical connection. They have lasted only a few seconds and then were gone. These long forgotten and well rid of memories that once claimed a part of me no longer survive. My wounds have healed, my essence returned, all parts of me now signed, sealed and delivered and welcomed home!

As for the voices on the other side that were talking as I was about to be "born", describing my life, what and how it would be like; it does not surprise me that we would be tutored on our way in. I say that because I have experienced it on the other end of life with family members and hospice patients alike, days before crossing over.

In the last days of my Mom's life, we would sit together outside on my sister's patio, quietly reading. She would all of a sudden look up, nod her head and say "He's back". Since it was just her and I sitting out there, my spirit's curiosity would kick right in and say "Who? Who is back?? Who is he? What does he look like?" She would give me that annoyed look of hers and say "I can't tell, his hat is pulled down over his eyes".

Maybe we are not meant to "see" their faces. I remember hearing the voices upon my rebirth and seeing outlines of robed figures with gray/white hair but no faces in particular.

Likewise, a few days before my mother- in- law passed away, we were in her living room. She had been napping in her chair and I was sitting on the couch reading. Again, it was just the two of us. She sat up with a startled look on her face and said "Grace, someone just told me my life was about to come to an end; or did I dream that?"

It only stands to reason then, if divine arrows are pointing our way into this life and also there to show the way out that they would certainly point the way for us in between. We just have to trust our instincts and let our spirits guide us; weaving the mysterious pieces of our lives—after all, they hold the pattern...

Ponderings

Do you think that maybe, just maybe, our spirits were only born into these physical bodies to see if they could find their way back to spirit? Maybe life is a test. Maybe, we are being tested for a higher life form; one that will become necessary when human beings defeat their own human purpose.

Consider the words "human beings"—**"HU"** is an ancient representation of the word **"GOD"**. "Beings" referring to something having an experience, something that exists. So, if human beings represent the physical existence of GOD in man then what might represent the spiritual existence? Maybe our physical experience here on Earth is just a stepping stone or a way back to our natural life form, which is one of spirit, or light. Maybe once we human beings become 'enlightened' we will become those beings of light. "Homo Luminous"—*light being*…is it closer than we think? Does it automatically happen when we "lighten up" and lose the tight grip on our physical, dense way of being? What if this is what we are all searching for, our own inner light; it cannot be found outside of ourselves, only within and maybe the reason for our physical life form is to find our way back to this light. *If so, then I suppose the darkness would have served its purpose…*

As I sit pen to paper, so many moons after I first began writing these poetic verses and ultimately this book, I am moved to a place of silence and stillness and with such gratitude for my experiences along the way and this opportunity to now share them with you. I gather up my closing thoughts and for the first time, begin to feel a tangible realization that I have finally come full circle. All those mornings of jotting down dream words, so many days when spirit took over and I kept writing aimless, endless poetry and so completely unabridged! Looking back now, I see how these experiences represent the roots of my soul journey—*sojourney,* so to speak.

Take "Cantilever" for instance, written about a black bear that I could not leave behind—*or was it about my own teddy bear that got thrown out at a very young age due to wear and tear that my heart still aches for? Or was it about being in a familiar ancient native village once again with my warrior brothers? Perhaps it was a visual road map pointing to the Pathfinders house which lies across the pines so far away and awakened in me, my sacred calling as a Bear Dancer? Maybe it was about my spirit guide who Sylvia Browne so aptly said without blinking an eye was named "Teddy".*

I often wonder about my George Harrison experience and if there is a more tangible connection. My full blooded Cherokee great grandmother's last name was Harris, close enough in the world of gematria for me! She has been my long standing confidante and guide in my native genealogical search, though she passed 10 years to the day before I was even born. I also see now, how this became my first conscious psychopomp experience—one that holds a high bar for all the ones I've experienced since and all the ones yet to come.

Then there is the curious synchronicity just found a few weeks ago. While looking through an old journal for a New Moon list *(things to be manifested)* that I had written, I noticed another list on the back page—web places that had caught my eye or workshops that I had been interested in. It shocked me to see the name "Ravenhawk" listed with just an Arkansas address, no website, no workshop. I wrote this in my journal YEARS before meeting Jim, who referred me to Julie (aka Ravenhawk) with whom I spent a few days with at her crystal shop and up on Mt Ida in search of crystals in Arkansas. Like I said, she and I had an immediate recognition upon meeting though we had never met before. *Or had we?*

There are several other synchronicities that have come to light after writing so many words and mysteriously penned poems, these I hold closest to my heart and soul to be shared only in spirit when the time is right.

As my thoughts return to the beginning, here, at the very end, I recognize the value of 'wanting' to find answers. We are each responsible for our own soul progress; only we can move ourselves forward on this journey. My soul yearned from a very young age and I've never stopped searching. My deep spirit connection trusted and kept following the spirit stones, seemingly laid at my feet. I can see now, how this has opened me up to a higher vibration or level of experience, one that is truly there for each and every one of us but we must first want it—our spirits must want out the physical door! Then and only then will we recognize the countless messages waiting to help us along the way.

There are no coincidences in life, only synchronicities—or what I like to call *"divine arrows"*. There is a reason I am writing this book just as there is a reason you are reading it. We are all just reflections of each other—some resonate and help push us forward with confidence on our chosen paths; some cast out reflections of improvement, even if only on a subconscious level, by seeing through another's eyes how we can make better choices, live better lives by becoming more 'like' them.

We only pass this way for a short while. All of our personal and collective human experiences are designed to help us grow; each bringing blessings and lessons. If we can learn to discern the ego from the spirit then we just might get out of our own way, detach from the dramas and dioramas of life and grow in the light towards more love, peace and harmony in the world. But like my search for my brother, we have to start somewhere. And hopefully, we will find answers and *ourselves* along the way, as the Divine Great Mystery intended it to be.

My wish for you having read this book is that you may feel the tug of perhaps just one tiny, gossamer thread and look up to see your own reflection in the mirror as my weaving touches upon yours—for we are all connected, many colors all woven into the great tapestry of life.

And who knows, perhaps "Cantilever" was simply just that—a message and reflection cast back through my brother's eyes, after all, Dad did call him "Little Bear"…and being heyoka, I know that divine arrows don't always have to point *forward*…

About the Author

Grace Walsh *is a Reiki Shamanism Master Teacher who lives on the South Shore of Boston at Nantasket with her husband Bill and Reiki cat, Taz.*

"Divine Arrows" represents her first written work and is a natural extension of her healing art classroom.

To contact or learn more please visit:

www.EarthenSpirit.org

Arrows of Gratitude

Many people come and go in our lives. It's true when they say that some stay a moment, some a season and perhaps some only for a certain reason. My guess is, initially anyway, we don't really know why they have arrived or why they have crossed our paths in the first place. One thing is certain, when I peer out through my multi-dimensional eyes, I realize (real eyes) that our human form is indeed like an onion. There are many layers to be peeled, if we choose! Who knows what sacred agreements we made with each other? When we find our path and continue to move from our heart center with only the highest intentions in mind, pathways begin to open up. Layers, if you will, of the onion, begin to expose the next layer underneath. Oftentimes, those layers make us cry. In my minds eye, I have come to know that life is indeed worth crying for! How else will we wash away the residue that blocks our truest vision? My vision has become clearer with the help of those I have journeyed with along the way; some for a moment, some in passing without conscious recognition and some for a very welcome, lifetime of seasons. I offer a small measure of gratitude here, to those whose eyes have looked into my own and the layers of clarity gained because of our crossing paths…

Platoon 245—http://www.wtv-zone.com/Platoon245USMC/index.html

Second Battalion First Marines—www.FirstMarines.org

Carol Bridges—http://www.sacredarts.info/

Raven Hail

Open Doors—http://www.opendoors7.com/

Mayan Majix—http://www.mayanmajix.com/

Bob Hunter—http://bobhuntermusic.com/

Sunray Meditation Society—http://www.sunray.org/

Jim Pathfinder Ewing—http://www.blueskywaters.com/

Annette Waya Ewing -
http://www.blueskywaters.com/animaltotemnecklaces.htm
http://www.blueskywaters.com/watercolor.html

Victor Wooten—www.victorwooten.com

Richard Cleveland—http://www.lovetheearth.com/

Julie Kincaid/Mt Ida—http://www.crystalseen.com/

Jen Desmond—http://balanceandbodyworkmassage.com/

Made in the USA
Charleston, SC
25 November 2012